Landscapes of
THE AZORES

a countryside guide

Fourth edition

Andreas Stieglitz

SUNFLOWER BOOKS

For my parents

Fourth edition © 2006
Sunflower Books™
PO Box 36160
London SW7 3WS, UK
www.sunflowerbooks.co.uk

Published in the USA by
Hunter Publishing Inc
130 Campus Drive
Edison, NJ 08818
www.hunterpublishing.com

ISBN 1-85691-308-2

Horse-drawn milk cart on São Miguel

Important note to the reader

I have tried to ensure that the descriptions and maps in this book are error-free at press date. The book will be updated, where necessary, whenever future printings permit. It will be very helpful for us to receive your comments (sent in care of the publishers, please) for the updating of future printings, and for the Update service described on the inside front cover of the book.

I also rely on those who use this book — especially walkers — to take along a good supply of common sense when they explore. Conditions change fairly rapidly on the Azores, and *storm damage or bulldozing may make a route unsafe at any time*. If the route is not as outlined here, and your way ahead is not secure, return to the point of departure. *Never attempt to complete a tour or walk under hazardous conditions!* Please read carefully the notes on pages 46-49, as well as the introductory comments at the beginning of each tour and walk (regarding road conditions, equipment, grade, distances and time, etc). Explore *safely*, while at the same time respecting the beauty of the countryside.

Cover photograph: Fajã da Caldeira de Santo Cristo (Walk 20, São Jorge)
Title page: view to Pico from a windmill on Faial

Photographs: Andreas Stieglitz
Maps by John Underwood, based on the 1:25,000 maps of the Serviço Cartográfico do Exército
A CIP catalogue record for this book is available from the British Library.
Printed and bound in England by J H Haynes & Co Ltd

Contents

4 Landscapes of the Azores

● Foreword ─────────────

The Azores … a mysterious-sounding name, evoking an unknown longing for distant shores. When I first got the idea of travelling to these islands, I pictured an archipelago floating in the middle of an azure-blue ocean. But where were they? I only knew their name from the weather reports, and I associated them with bright blue skies and a lot of sunshine. The Portuguese explorers of the 15th century sailed a long and perilous course to the Azores, some 1500 kilometres — almost a thousand miles — from Lisbon, on their way to the New World. These seafarers apparently named the Azores after the many buzzards there; they mistook them for hawks, which are called *açores* in Portuguese.

There are nine islands far out in the Atlantic Ocean, all of them of volcanic origin. The Azores rise above sea level from a depth of several thousand metres. They are not the remains of the legendary continent of Atlantis, which is said to have sunk in the ocean once upon a time. Nonetheless, there is an aura of mystery about this lush green archipelago … awe-inspiring mountains and peaceful valleys with abundant exotic plants, enchanting lakes of stunning beauty amidst extinct craters, charming hill country with fields and meadows, spectacular hydrangea hedges criss-crossing the landscape, and magnificent coasts lined by picturesque villages and historical towns.

Here the highest mountain in all Portugal, Pico, rises some 2351 metres (7700 feet) above sea level on the island which bears its name; on Graciosa there is a subterranean crater lake at the bottom of a huge cavern; and in the basin of Furnas on São Miguel you will see mud cauldrons, small geysers and hot rocks. The evergreen, park-like landscapes of the Azores are full of surprises and invite the visitor to explore — a dream world for anyone seeking unspoilt nature, tranquillity and the chance to 'get back to basics'.

And then there are the gentle people: friendly and helpful, with a genuine interest in the strangers visiting their secluded world. Anyone who comes here once will certainly be fascinated enough to want to return. — ANDREAS STIEGLITZ

Some words of thanks

I would like to thank all my friends who patiently accompanied me on many walks and made the 'work' even more enjoyable. Many thanks to Rui Pavão, my helpful taxi driver on São Miguel, to Angelo Neto, my taxi driver on São Jorge, and to Silvio Medina on Flores. Thanks also to João Xavier, on whom I rely as a taxi driver on Pico. I am also grateful to Renate Rahäuser from Horta, Faial, for her assistance. Once again, I would like to thank the publisher, Pat Underwood, for her unflagging enthusiasm, which has made this book possible. Last, but not least, *muito obrigado* to all Açoreanos for their helpfulness!

Useful books

Pierluigi Bragaglia: *Walker's Guide to Lajes/Santa Cruz old footpaths* (two volumes) explores the whole network of old footpaths on Flores in detail, including precise walk descriptions. The books contain a wealth of historical and other background information; they are available on the island.

Hanno Schäfer: *Flora of the Azores*, published (in English) in 2002 by Margraf Verlag (www.margraf-verlag.de), is the most comprehensive guide to the wildflowers of the Azores, describing 650 plants with many full-colour photographs.

Erik Sjögren: *Plants and Flowers of the Azores* (English/German/Portuguese), published 2001, describes about 100 plants, with photographs.

David Sayers: *Azores*, published by Bradt Publications, is the only dedicated general guide in English.

Useful addresses

Regional tourist office of the Azores

Direcção Regional de Turismo
Rua Ernesto Rebelo, 14
9900 Horta, Faial
Tel: 00351 292 200500
Fax: 200501/2
e-mail: acoresturismo
@mail.telepac.pt

Portuguese tourist office in the UK

Portuguese Trade & Tourism Office
22-25A Sackville Street
London W1X 1DE
Tel: 020-7494 1441
Fax: 020-7494 1868

Local tourist offices

Note that all the tourist offices are closed on weekends and public holidays. The international dialing code for Portugal is 00-351.

Faial: Posto de Turismo
Rua Vasco da Gama
9900 Horta, Faial
Tel: 292 292237
Fax: 292 292006

Flores: Posto de Turismo
9580 Santa Cruz das Flores
Tel: 292 52369

Graciosa: Posto de Turismo
Largo Vasco da Gama
9980 Santa Cruz, Graciosa
Tel: 295 712509
Fax: 295 712124

Pico: Posto de Turismo
Rua Conselheiro Terra Pinheiro
9950 Madalena, Pico
Tel: 292 623524
Fax: 292 622500

Santa Maria: Posto de Turismo*
Aeroporto
9560 Vila do Porto, Santa Maria

Tel: 296 886355,
Fax: 296 886528
*open only when planes arrive and depart

São Jorge: Posto de Turismo
Rua Conselheiro Dr José Pereira
9880 Velas, São Jorge
Tel: 295 412440,
Fax: 295 412333

São Miguel: Delegação de Turismo
Avenida Infante Don Henrique
9500 Ponta Delgada, São Miguel
Tel: 296 285743,
Fax: 296 282211

Terceira: Delegação de Turismo
Rua Direita 70-74
9700 Angra, Terceira
Tel: 295 213393
Fax: 295 212922

Web sites focussing on the Azores

You will find the Azores in cyberspace, as well as mid-Atlantic! Below are two major sites (for flights and ferries see page 7).

www.stieglitz.info (with an English version) is the author's homepage with up-to-date information on the Azores and other destinations, including many links

www.drtacores.pt is the homepage of the Azores Tourism Department (with many foreign language versions)

Introduction

How to get there

TAP Air Portugal (www.tap.pt) offers daily flights from London Heathrow to São Miguel, Faial and Terceira, but all are via Lisbon. Several tour operators have package holidays to the Azores; contact the Portuguese Tourism Office (details opposite). Alternatively, you can book charter flights to/from Lisbon and ongoing travel with SATA, the archipelago's regional airline (www.sata.pt). SATA handles all flights within the Azores, serving all nine islands at least once a day with small turboprop planes. Information about special prices (eg the Azores Airpass) for island-hopping and up-to-date flight schedules are also shown on the SATA web page. All flights should be reconfirmed in advance.

All islands belonging to the central group are also served by ferries operating according to set schedules. In the summer season, these are a good alternative to taking a plane. Not only are they considerably cheaper, but it's fun approaching an island by sea and, if you're lucky, you may even spot whales or dolphins. Moreover, all ferries moor right in the harbour of the capital town of each island, so you don't have to take taxis from and back to the airport. Sailings between Horta (Faial) and Madalena (Pico) are frequent (see 'Pico Ferry' timetable on page 134), so you can stay on Faial even if you want to take day trips to Pico, saving you the trouble of changing hotels. But ferries from the central group to the eastern and western groups of the archipelago are very rare or non-existent. Furthermore, these sailings take a lot of time, so a SATA flight is usually a better option. Up-to-date timetables for the Transmaçor ferry company can be accessed on the web: www.transmacor.pt.

Getting about on the islands

São Miguel, Terceira, Graciosa, Pico and Faial have an extensive **public bus** network. The walks in this book are planned so that in many cases you can use these buses for access and return. It's advisable to get to the bus stop in good time — the bus drivers keep very tight schedules! If you want to be picked up by a passing bus, you have to *give a clear hand signal — even when waiting at a bus stop.* To let the bus driver know that you want to get off at the next stop, just ring the bell. Note that bus stops are not always clearly marked. Tickets are generally sold on the bus. You will find timetables for the buses you need for the walks on page 134.

If you prefer, **cars** can easily be hired on all the islands (except Corvo). Fully comprehensive insurance is strongly recommended.

Generally you must pay a deposit before taking the car (except for payments made by credit card). Make sure that the car is in good condition, too, before taking it out on the roads; any damage should be recorded in the contract.

Taxis are a good alternative to hiring a car, especially for short distances. When a taxi is your only option for transport at the end of a walk, be sure to arrange this in advance with a taxi driver (or ask your hotel to arrange it). Taxis can also be hired for an entire day — for touring an island, for example; again, ask your hotel to find an English-speaking driver for you. Taxis are cream-coloured; there are taxi ranks in all towns. Fares depend on the distance driven; the price is either metered or looked up in the official price list (but it is always a good idea to enquire about the fare prior to the journey). Remember, too, that on longer journeys outside the towns you will be charged not only for the distance driven with you as a passenger in the taxi, but also for the distance the taxi driver travels from or back to his base.

Where to stay

Many tourists travel to the Azores on package holidays, to take advantage of the 'all-in' prices. Of course you can also book flight and accommodation separately: consult the tourist information offices to find accommodation, but bear in mind that during the summer, especially in July and August, many hotels are fully booked due to their limited capacity and the high demand. So book well in advance if you are planning to visit the Azores during the peak season. Addresses of local tourist information offices are given on page 6.

Basically your choice of accommodation is between standard hotels, former manor houses that have been converted into hotels (usually very stylish and set in particularly pleasant surroundings), *pensãos* and *residencials* (almost as comfortable as hotels, but less expensive) and holiday homes and apartments. Holiday homes *(turismo rural)*, which are often old stone cottages that have been lovingly renovated, are becoming more and more popular, since they offer solitude in quiet and peaceful surroundings. They are frequently rented out privately. However, most of these holiday homes are located out in the country so you really need a hire car.

Eastern group: Of all the islands in the Azores, **São Miguel** offers the best range of accommodation in the different categories. Most hotels are located in Ponta Delgada, the ideal base for walks around the island if you depend on public transport. Some people might find the city too noisy and hectic, with a lot of traffic in the streets during the day. There are other hotels around the island for those seeking more seclusion and quiet, for instance the Hotel Terra Nostra in Furnas, which is pleasantly located in the eponymous park. The Convento in Vila Franca is a former monastery that has been turned into a very tasteful and discreet hotel in idyllic surroundings. On **Santa Maria**, there is a hotel in Vila do Porto and some other lodgings, for instance the Apartments Mar e Sol in a beautiful sandy bay on the south coast.

Central group: Angra do Heroísmo, the charming capital city of **Terceira**, offers a range of hotels. On **Graciosa**, there are two *residencials* in the capital, Santa Cruz. On **São Jorge**, there are some hotels and *residencials* in the capital, Velas, as well as the Quinta do Canavial on the outskirts. On **Pico**, there are places to stay in Madalena, Cais/São Roque and Lajes. On **Faial**, nearly all accommodation is located in Horta, the capital. On the last three islands you will also find beautiful holiday homes.

Western group: On **Flores**, there is accommodation in Santa Cruz. The west of the island is even more quiet and unspoilt. The Residencial Argonauta, an old house in Fajã Grande that has been tastefully renovated, is very pleasant. Aldeia da Cuada is an old hamlet with stone houses carefully converted into holiday homes for those seeking solitude and quiet. **Corvo** has no accommodation.

Climate and weather

The Azores are characterised by a mild subtropical ocean climate, favoured by the warm waters of the Gulf Stream. In summer, when the Azorean high hovers over the archipelago, the warm and humid air rises during the day, causing clouds to gather around the summits, while there is usually bright sunshine on the coast. In winter, when the area of high pressure moves to the south, its antagonist, the Iceland low, occasionally gets a grip on the Azores, accompanied by stormy winds and strong rainfall!

The average daily temperatures at Ponta Delgada are 17°C/63°F in January and 25°C/77°F in July. But in contrast to these pleasant temperatures, the islands are quite humid — on many days, the humidity ranges between 75% and 90%! This sultry atmosphere is oppressive for some people, but plants seem to enjoy it. The position of the Azores, in the middle of the Atlantic, ensures that the humid ocean air falls as abundant rain on the islands — they are not so green all year round for nothing! The precipitation increases on the archipelago from east to west; at Santa Cruz on Flores there is twice as much rain as at Ponta Delgada on São Miguel.

But weather conditions are hardly ever the same on all parts of any island. If you know from which direction the wind is blowing, you may well escape the clouds by finding a sunny corner on the island — in the lee of the wind or by the coast.

May through August are generally the best months to visit the Azores. The weather is mostly stable, with little rain and a lot of sunshine. Above all, hydrangeas will be at their best from mid-June onward. During the rest of year, the weather tends to be changeable, with occasional fierce storms blowing over the islands. Nonetheless, you can enjoy perfect days with bright sunshine and a deep blue sky at any time of the year.

Language

Portuguese is the language of the islands — sometimes as a strong dialect. But you don't have to study Portuguese before you go there — the younger Azoreans learn English at school, and among the older people there are many former emigrants who have returned from North America and speak English well. Nonetheless, it is quite a good idea to memorise some important Portuguese words and phrases, as there are always situations where nobody speaks a foreign language. Take special care to pronounce the place names correctly — the bus drivers, especially, will be very grateful! Portuguese pronunciation is rather complicated and differs considerably from the spelling, but you can, for example, ask someone at the reception in your hotel to help you with pronunciation.

People on the Azores usually say hello when they pass you out in the country and when they go into a bar or shop. Tourists should respond in a similarly friendly manner.

Important questions and phrases (stressed vowels are in bold type):

English	Portuguese	approximate pronunciation
Good morning	bom dia	bohng **dee**-ah
Good afternoon	boa tarde	boa **tar**-de
Good evening	boa noite	boa **noy**-te
Please/Thank you	por favor/obrigado	por fa-**vohr**/o-bree-**gah**-doh
Yes/No	sim/não	sengh/nowg
I understand/don't —	percebo/não percebo	per-**see**-boo/**nowg** per-**see**-boo
Do you understand?	percebe?	per-**se**-beh?
Speak slowly!	fale devagar!	**fa**-leh de-va-**gar**
I am ill	estou doente	ish-**too** do-**ayn**-teh
I am hurt	estou ferido	ish-**too** feh-**ree**-doh
It's urgent	é urgente	ay oor-**shen**-teh
Please help me	ajude-me	ah-**shu**-deh may
Police	polícia	po-lee-**see**-a
Where is ...	onde está ...	**on**-deh esh-**ta** ...
a telephone?	um telefone?	oongh tele-**foh**-neh?
a toilet?	um lavatório?	oongh la-va-**toh**-ree-o
men's toilet?	homens?	**oh**-mengs?
ladies' toilet?	mulheres?	muhl-**yare**-esh?
a restaurant?	um restaurante?	oongh rish-tau-**ran**-teh?
a chemist?	uma farmácia?	oongh far-ma-**see**-a?
a doctor?	um médico?	oongh **may**-dee-koo?
How much does it cost?	quanto custa?	**kwang**-to kush-tah?
Big/Little	grande/pequeno	**gran**-day/pe-**kay**-noo
No entry	entrada proibida	in-**tra**-da pro-ee-**bee**-da
Watch out!	atenção!	ah-ten-**saough**!
Open/Closed	aberto/fechado	ah-**bear**-toh/fe-**scha**-doh
I'd like to eat/drink	quero comer/beber	**ke**-roo koo-**mer**/bay-**bear**
Where does	Onde va	**on**-deh va
this bus go?	isto autocarro?	**ish**-to au-to-**kar**-roo?
Does this bus go to ...?	Va isto autocarro a ...?	Va **ish**-to au-to-**kar**-roo a ...?
Which bus goes to ...?	Que autocarro va a...?	**Kay** au-to-**kar**-roo va a ...?
When does this	Quando parte	**Kwan**-do **par**-teh
bus leave?	isto autocarro?	**ish**-to au-to-**kar**-roo?

Words frequently found on maps

cabeço — mound, summit
caldeira — basin, volcanic crater
canada — trail
fajã — (coastal) plain, landslip
farol — lighthouse
grota — small gorge
igreja — church
lagoa — mountain or crater lake
lomba — mountain ridge
lombada — mountain spine

mata — wood
miradouro — viewpoint
monte — mountain
morro — hill
pico — peak, summit
praia — beach
quinta — manor house
ribeira — stream, river
serra — mountain chain
vila — small town

Geology and vulcanology

The Azores (and all other islands in the Atlantic) are of volcanic origin. The archipelago is located on top of the mid-Atlantic fault running along the ocean floor between Europe and Africa on one side and America on the other. This is an extremely active zone geologically, where the earth's crust is steadily being pulled apart between the tectonic plates on their continental drift, and blazing, molten magma surges up. The cooling magma gradually builds a submarine mountain ridge, with its highest peaks — in this case, the Azores — eventually rising above sea level.

On most Azorean islands, the landscape is characterised by cone-shaped volcanoes (strato-volcanoes) which have alternately thrown up ashes and lava, eventually piling up layers of soft tuff and solid lava. In many cases, the typical volcanic craters or *caldeiras* (literally 'cauldrons') have thus evolved. A *caldeira* is created by the explosion and subsequent collapse of the original cone-shaped volcano. Usually a lake appears at the bottom of the crater basin, and the high walls of the crater plummet steeply to the basin, whereas the external walls slope more gently.

Nature has not yet come to a rest on the Azores. The tectonic plates on which the islands sit are steadily drifting apart — the eastern and central group some 1.5cm (0.625") per year to the east, Flores and Corvo at about the same rate to the west. So the constant stress on the continental crust doesn't come as a surprise. But this gradual movement only registers on seismographs; only the strong, jerky upheavals are felt as a shaking and trembling of the ground.

Apart from Santa Maria, Flores and Corvo, earthquakes have been reported on all the islands since historical times. Particularly strong earthquakes in recent years occurred in 1980, when Angra do Heroísmo on Terceira was severely damaged, and in 1998, when the entire central group was hit and devastation was worst on Faial. Eruptions, too, have taken place repeatedly — the most recent being in 1957/58 on Faial. Such natural disasters have given cause to massive emigration in the past. Modern houses and older buildings that have been restored are mostly built to withstand earthquakes. Unfortunately, the beautiful old houses built of drystone walls remain particularly vulnerable.

Vegetation

When the Portuguese explorers of the 15th century steered a course to the Azores, they discovered uninhabited islands covered with dense evergreen woods. Settlement soon began to change the appearance of the landscape, with cultivation forcing back the natural woodlands. Just five percent of the Azores, mostly impassable mountain regions, steep gorges and inaccessible craters, is still covered with native vegetation. Some 56 species are endemic to the islands, which means they are growing under natural conditions only here and nowhere else in the world.

In the coastal zones (up to about 300m/1000ft above sea level), where the relatively-dry climate favours human settlement, numerous species have been introduced by man over the centuries, displacing the native vegetation. Under natural conditions, the Azorean candleberry tree or wax myrtle (*Myrica faya*; Portuguese *faia*) thrives in this region. This evergreen tree produces edible black wrinkled berries. It is now threatened by cheese wood or Victorian laurel (*Pittosporum undulatum*), originally native to Australia. This tree was probably introduced as shelter for orange trees and originally only grown in high dense hedgerows. Nowadays, it is widely distributed below 500m/1650ft, having expelled *faia* in most places.

The native vegetation of the Azores in the moist and misty cloud zone (above 500m/1650ft) is dominated by laurel or bay (*Laurus azorica*; Portuguese *louro*), juniper (*Juniperus brevifolia*; Portuguese *cedro-do-mato*) and tree heather (*Erica azorica*; Portuguese *urze*). These endemics grow in dense bushy woodland rich in various mosses. This unique laurel-juniper forest, dependent on moist air, has been mostly expelled through clearance and ever-expanding pastureland. Only on São Miguel, Pico and Terceira can these endemic woodlands still be found.

Another immigrant is Madeira mahogany (*Persea indica*; Portuguese *vinhático*), native to the Canary Islands and Madeira and introduced to the Azores some 300 years ago. Growing in altitudes above 200m/650ft, this tree, a member of the avocado family, is prized for its beautiful reddish-brown wood reminiscent of mahogany.

Massive reafforestation has been taking place since the 1860s, with the planting of Japanese cedars (*Cryptomeria japonica*), an attractive, fast-growing conifer with reddish bark that was originally native to Japan. Unfortunately, its fallen needles accumulate on the ground and stifle the growth of any other plants. Some 250,000 specimens of this commercially-important tree are cut per year; more than twice that number is replanted.

The Azores' most typical plant, the famed hydrangea (*Hydrangea macrophylla*; Portuguese *hortensia*) is also native to Japan. When it starts flowering in June, the colourful hedgerows enclosing pastures are a spectacular sight.

The islands in detail

The nine islands of the Azores are widely spread in the North Atlantic (see touring map). The archipelago consists of the eastern group (São Miguel and Santa Maria), the central group (Terceira, Graciosa, São Jorge, Pico and Faial) and the western group (Flores and Corvo). Some 650km (400mi) separate the most distant islands, Santa Maria and Corvo! In 1976, the Azores were granted the status of an autonomous region by Portugal, with their own flag (nine stars forming a semicircle around a hawk on a blue and white ground). The regional government resides in Ponta Delgada on São Miguel; the regional parliament meets in Horta on Faial. The archipelago has around 237,000 inhabitants, most of whom live on São Miguel (53%) and Terceira (23.5%).

Almost everywhere on the Azores cows can be seen grazing the lush pastures, testifying to the importance of livestock and dairy farming. The excellent Azorean cheese (especially the one from São Jorge) and beef are important export products. Cereals and field crops are nowadays only rarely grown, except for maize. Although this is mainly used as cattle fodder, be sure to sample some of the compact, moist and slightly sweet corn bread (pão de milho) which is sold in most bakeries. Some special crops are still grown on São Miguel: tobacco (on the humid northern coast), tea (the only two tea plantations in Western Europe are near the village of Gorreana) and pineapple (see panel page 30). The deep waters around the Azores are rich in fish, yet fishing does not play an important role and is aimed only at meeting local demand.

São Miguel ('Saint Michael') is the largest and perhaps most varied of the islands — an ideal place to get a first impression of the archipelago, but equally suitable for several weeks' holiday. Because of its size (760 km²; 293 sq mi), its population (140,000) and its economic importance, it is considered the main island in the archipelago. The coastline is rocky and consists mostly of steep cliffs. The north coast is generally harsher and rougher than the more gentle south coast, which in

GINGER LILY
Numerous exotic plants introduced by man thrive well in the sultry Azorean climate, thus posing a severe threat to the native vegetation. The ginger lily (Hedychium gardnerianum), originally confined to the Himalaya, spreads aggressively by massive rhizomatous growth, expelling any other plants at altitudes between 150-600m.
Starting at the end of July, the big yellow-orange flowers that bloom in long spikes make it a very attractive ornamental plant that easily lets you forget the ecological impact the invasion of the ginger lily has on the native vegetation.
If you pull out one of the flowers and suck out the stalk, you will taste delicious honey-sweet ginger.

places looks almost Mediterranean, with some scattered sandy bays. Ponta Delgada, the busy capital, is the biggest town in the Azores. It has a beautiful old town, where black and white buildings predominate. A fine example of this style is the Manueline doorway of the 16th-century parish church of São Sebastião. Well worth a visit is the Museu Carlos Machado in the former monastery of Santo André, focussing on the culture and history of the Azores.

Like all the other Atlantic islands, São Miguel is of volcanic origin — something most visitors don't usually think about on arrival, since the island glows with lush green colours (from whence the epithet 'Ilha Verde' or 'Green Island'). São Miguel consists of separate volcanic massifs which have only gradually grown together to form one large island. The east is the oldest part of the island (3-4 million years) — the Serra da Tronqueira, with its many gorges and the island's highest mountain, Pico da Vara (1103m/ 3618ft). This is secluded, scarcely-populated countryside, with extensive forests and high-lying pastures, often shrouded in mist and difficult to reach. The central part of São Miguel rises around the Serra de Água de Pau, a huge volcanic massif culminating in the Pico da Barrosa (947m/ 3106ft). At the bottom of its basin lies the Lagoa do Fogo ('Fire Lake'; see panel page 60), with its pale, fine-pumice beach.

At the geological borderline between these two mountain ranges, two great caldeiras have evolved in more recent times: the basin of Povoação and the adjacent basin of Furnas, with its idyllic village and

These extremely narrow walled-in lanes are typical of the area north of Ponta Delgada on São Miguel.

lake. Here there are many volcanic phenomena — hot springs, mud cauldrons and hot rocks.

The western part of São Miguel is dominated by the famous Caldeira das Sete Cidades, a huge crater basin with the twin lakes Lagoa Azul and Lagoa Verde, one blue, one green, at its bottom. The youngest part of the island, geologically speaking, lies in the east between Ponta Delgada and Ribeira Grande — the low *pico*-zone. This land 'bridge' connected the separate parts of the island some 50,000 years ago; it is studded with about 65 small volcanic craters which have been active for the last 5000 years. The most recent eruption occurred in 1652, when Pico do Fogo north of Vila da Lagoa breathed fire.

Santa Maria is the oldest island in the archipelago; its volcanic activity ceased a long time ago, and so it lacks the landforms typical on the other islands. Apart from volcanic rock, there is also lime-stone, clay and even 3,000,000 year-old fossils from the Tertiary Period; these are not found on any of the other islands. Santa Maria's climate is also different — it is the driest island and often called the 'Sunny Island' or the 'Algarve of the Azores'. If you are planning to visit the Azores in winter, Santa Maria is a very good choice. Blessed by the sun, many plants start blooming in February, including Victorian laurel with its honey-sweet blossoms, azaleas, cala lilies and montbretias.

Vast plains extend across the west of Santa Maria — open pastureland, parched in summer but lush and green in winter. Here there is also the island's airport with its huge airstrip (the obligatory stop-over on trans-Atlantic flights until the 1960s). A wooded mountain ridge rises in the centre of the island, culminating in Pico Alto (587m/1925ft). In the east there is charming green hill country.

The population comprises a mere 6000 inhabitants. Apart from the main town of Vila do Porto with its beautiful churches and the Fort São Brás, there are some enchanting villages. Typical houses with tall chimneys and red-tiled roofs are scattered over rolling hills and valleys. Santa Maria has other attractions, too — like magnificent bays bordered by some golden sandy beaches. Those in search of a peaceful, rather small island with attractive landscapes will be richly rewarded.

Terceira — the name means 'Third' (ie, the third island in the archipelago to be discovered) — consists of several large volcanic massifs, their huge rims manifesting themselves as extended mountain ridges *(serras)*. The highest of these, the Serra de Santa Bárbara (1021m/3349ft) in the west, was last active in 1762. On the coast, steep cliffs predominate; access to the sea is only rarely possible. The island has a population of 58,000.

All settlements on Terceira stretch along the coastal roads, running through an almost treeless countryside of pastureland and fields subdivided by a plethora of stone walls. The unpopulated interior of the island can only be reached on a few roads; it rises to more than 400m/1200ft and is often enveloped in clouds — a strangely wild and rugged landscape. In the expanse of the highlands there are still some large, jungle-like areas of brushwood covered with typical scrub vegetation — tree heather, juniper and mosses. However, Terceira is not easy to explore off the asphalt roads, since there are very few suitable footpaths.

The well-kept capital city of Angra do Heroísmo has been included by UNESCO as an outstanding historical monument in the World Heritage list. With its fine palaces, houses, churches and monasteries, Angra is undoubtedly the most beautiful town on the Azores. Systematically laid out as a fortified port on the trans-Atlantic route in the 16th and 17th century, it is a perfect example of Renaissance urban planning.

Graciosa, the 'Gracious', is the second smallest island (62km²; 24 sq mi) in the archipelago. Gently sloping mountain ridges (*serras*) and rounded hilltops mould its landscapes. The maximum altitude of 398m/1035ft is the lowest of the group, which explains the relatively low precipitation. On Graciosa, you can expect more sunshine (or at least less rain) than on the other islands of the central group.

Graciosa has a population of 5000 inhabitants. Due to its relatively dry climate, Graciosa's villages are not restricted to the coastal areas, but are scattered all over the island. The fertile land is mainly used for farming, being subdivided by numerous black stone walls. The windmills with their red bonnets are especially charming; many of them have been renovated in recent years. The small, tidy capital of Santa Cruz illustrates why Graciosa was given the name 'White Island': its houses are traditionally whitewashed. Apart from some beautiful churches, the Museum of Folklore with its interesting collection of agricultural utensils and whaling boats merits a visit.

Graciosa's *caldeira*, a huge volcanic crater, rises in the southeast of the island. This crater holds one of the most important tourist attractions in the archipelago: inside it is the Furna do Enxofre ('Sulphur Cavern'), a huge cave with an underground crater lake at its bottom.

São Jorge ('Saint George'; 10,000 inhabitants) is, for many visitors to the Azores, *the* great discovery … for good reason. This unique island culminates in a mountain ridge 56km/35mi long and up to 8km/6mi wide. It rises very steeply from the sea and consists of numerous peaks which run in an almost straight line. The gentle high-mountain region lies at an altitude of 300-700m (1000-2300ft) and plummets down to the ocean quite abruptly, particularly on the north coast — a truly magnificent sight.

Almost all São Jorge's villages are set on small coastal plains (*fajãs;* see panel page 104) below these tall cliffs, and some hamlets

São Jorge: Caldeira de Cima (Walk 20); opposite: windmill on Graciosa

can only be reached via narrow footpaths. The little-populated highlands are often shrouded in mist, especially in the winter. São Jorge's main town is Velas, where you can experience an eerie theatrical performance after sunset: Cory's Shearwater *(Calonectris diomedea;* Portuguese *cagarras;* see panel page 95) circle at the cliffs opposite the port at night, with haunting chuckling and mewing calls. The church of Santa Bárbara in Manadas, with its carved cedar ceiling, is considered one of the most beautiful baroque churches on the islands. The church tower in Urzelina, rising on top of a lava flow dating from an eruption in 1808, is also worth seeing.

Besides its glorious natural setting, São Jorge affords — like no other island of the central group — magnificent views of the neighbouring islands. Old paths along the steep coast and some new cinder tracks in the highlands provide some of the most rewarding walks on the Azores.

Pico, the second largest island in the archipelago (447km²; 173 sq mi), is dominated by its huge eponymous volcanic cone. Rising to 2351m/7711ft above sea level, Pico is the highest mountain on the Azores and in the whole of Portugal. The height and sheer walls of this truly majestic volcano — one of the most beautiful in the world — are hard to appreciate when you are close to it; they are far better judged when the mountain is seen from a distance (see photograph page 24). However, Pico has more to offer the visitor than just its main peak; the geological backbone extends quite a long way to the east, where many volcanoes are strung along in a line, at an average altitude of 800m/2600ft; hidden away in their hollows are small lakes.

Up until recent times, the western and central parts of Pico were subject to violent volcanic eruptions, with subsequent floods of lava covering the landscape. Very little soil has so far developed in these harsh rocky regions (called *mistérios*). Untouched by man, natural woodlands have spread in these areas. In the coastal regions especially, the lava fields have often been cleared so the land could be cultivated. The myriad rocks were used to build numerous dry-stone walls forming sheltered enclosures (see panel page 114), or else piled into *maroiços* (stone heaps).

The island has a population of 15,000. The main town is Madalena, from where there are frequent ferries to Horta. Lajes do Pico was a whaling centre for many centuries (see panel page 88), and the Museu dos Baleeiros (Whalers' Museum) at Lajes is an interesting place to visit. Pico's men were reputed to be particularly courageous whalers; Herman Melville's 'Moby Dick' is set in the waters off the Azores. Nowadays one can join whale-watching boat trips organised by different companies.

Faial (from *faia*, the endemic *Myrica faya* or wax myrtle) rises almost symmetrically on all sides, gently ascending from the coast to the Caldeira. The highest peak on the island, Cabeço Gordo, rises to 1043m/3421ft near the rim of the crater. On the coast, steep cliffs alternate with some pleasant sandy bays. The eastern part of the island has charming countryside with gentle slopes and ridges, and friendly villages nestling in the valleys.

A chain of small volcanic cones runs from the Caldeira along to the west. This is the geological backbone of the island — a green, but rather harsh and little-

Flores: waterfall at the Poço do Bacalhau (Walk 29)

populated region. The Vulcão dos Capelinhos emerged from the sea in 1957/58 just at the end of this line of volcanoes, in a violent eruption that enlarged the western tip of the island by 2.4 square kilometres (see panel page 44). Nowhere on the Azores is the impact of an eruption more forcefully evident than here.

Faial has a population of 15,000. For many centuries, the lively capital city of Horta was the most important stop for ships sailing between Europe and America. Even today transatlantic yachts arrive from all over the world, each crew commemorating their journey by painting a picture on the famous harbour mole. Peter's Café Sport on the esplanade is the legendary place where all the skipper meet in the evening — and seamen's yarns are spun.

When the first submarine cable was laid from Portugal to Horta in 1893, the town began to develop as the centre of trans-Atlantic communication. All transatlantic cables, after thousands of kilometres underwater, came ashore here for amplification of their signals. It is worthwhile visiting the Museum of Horta (housed in the Palácio do Colégio, the former Jesuits' college) and the old whaling factory at Porto Pim.

Flores and **Corvo** are the most westerly outposts of Europe in the Atlantic. Actually, these two islands are already part of the New World, since geologically they are situated on the American shelf, gradually drifting westward.

Flores ('Flowers'; 4000 inhabitants) abounds in lush vegetation. It is the most humid island of the Azores; this is evident not only in the high amount of precipitation, but also in the sultry atmosphere. Low clouds, stormy winds and strong rainfalls may occur at any time of the year, even in summer. The unpredictable weather may well affect the SATA flight schedule, but the magnificent landscape is reward enough for any delay in getting there!

The geological structure of Flores differs from the other islands in the archipelago, resulting in some magnificent landscapes: basalt predominates, in the form of high-lying plateaus where waterfalls plummet down over vertical drops. Sheer cliffs along the coasts, steep escarpments and deep gorges alternate, with bizarre rock formations like the Rocha dos Bordões (photograph page 125) punctuating the landscape. On the high-mountain region in the island's interior, enchanting lakes hide in some of the crater basins. The wild and romantic atmosphere is further enhanced by the mist often prevailing on the upper elevations — an almost eerie sight.

Corvo (literally 'Raven', but actually the cormorant, *Corvus marinus*, is meant) is the smallest (17km²; 7 sq mi) and quietest island in the archipelago — a single volcanic crater rising abruptly from the sea (photograph page 133). Only the southern slopes ease gently down to Vila Nova, the only village (with a mere 400 inhabitants). The feeling of solitude which Corvo evokes is heightened by the 'unreal' impression you have when viewing its fantastic crater basin. When you visit Flores, *do* spend a day on Corvo.

Picnicking

The varied landscapes of the Azores provide good opportunities for picnics. Shady woodlands are often the setting for a 'Parque Florestal' — an organised picnic site. Most of these have been charmingly laid out, with tables, benches and fireplaces, washing facilities and toilets. There are also picnic tables and benches at many viewpoints along the roads; signs alert you to these lookout points with their name ('Miradouro …'). All organised picnic places along the routes of the car tours are indicated on the touring maps and in the touring notes by the symbol ⌱.

On the following five pages I suggest some particularly pleasant picnic spots. A map reference is given in most cases: many of these picnics lie along walking routes, and the location of the picnic spot is mentioned in the car touring notes and indicated on the relevant large-scale *walking map* by the symbol *P*, while 🚌 and 🚗 symbols on the map show the nearest access by bus or car.

You can buy everything you need for your picnic at local markets or in supermarkets. Fresh fruit and vegetables are available all year round, for instance the small aromatic bananas grown on the Azores. The famous cheese is very tasty too. For bread there is a choice between different kinds of wheat bread and the heavier, moister corn bread *(pão de milho)* — don't miss it! While the wines imported from the Portuguese mainland (eg Dão) are far superior, the rougher local wines (made on Pico, Terceira, Graciosa and Santa Maria) may just be right for a picnic. Good mineral water is bottled on the Azores, so you don't have to buy water imported from mainland Portugal.

Remember to wear stout shoes if you have to walk any distance, and take a sunhat. **All picnickers should read the country code on page 48 and go quietly in the countryside.**

View from Vista do Rei to the Lagoa Azul and Lagoa Verde (Picnics 2-5)

1 SÃO MIGUEL: PONTA DOS MOSTEIROS (map pages 52-53, photo page 51)

🚌 bus to Mosteiros: 35min on foot

🚗 car: 35min on foot. Park in front of the church in Mosteiros.

Whether you come by bus or car, walk northeast along the main road in Mosteiros and turn left after some 350 metres/yards into Rua da Eira. After the last houses, descend steps on the left to the pebble beach. You can also continue along the track to see more dramatic rock formations. Turn right at the next fork and follow the village road straight back to the church.

This short walk leads you along the jagged rocky coast of Mosteiros with its pebble beaches, natural pools and strange brown and black lava rock formations — a wonderful place for a picnic. No facilities and **no shade**.

2 SÃO MIGUEL: LAGOA AZUL/SETE CIDADES (map p 52-53, photo opposite) 🅿

🚌 bus to Sete Cidades: 5min on foot. Get off the bus at the church in the village and follow the road straight down to the lake and picnic site.

🚗 car: no walking. Park beside the lake.

This is an organised picnic site on the shores of the Lagoa Azul ('Blue Lake'), with tables and benches. **Little shade.**

3 SÃO MIGUEL: LAGOA AZUL/CERRADO DAS FREIRAS (map pages 52-53, photographs opposite and page 58) 🅿

🚌 bus to Sete Cidades: 50min on foot. Follow the notes for Walk 2 to the bridge that connects the shores of the twin lakes (20min), then see below.

🚗 car: no walking. Drive to the wood on the eastern shore of the Blue Lake.

Approaching from Sete Cidades, a gravel road turns off left just beyond the bridge and runs along the eastern shore of the 'Blue Lake' (Lagoa Azul), past a camp site on a small spit of land. The steep walls of the crater recede here, and there are a few cottages (Cerrado das Freiras) between hilly fields and pastures. At the end of the gravel road (2.3km), where a stream flows from a side valley into the lake, you come upon a small wood — perfect for picnicking under trees (some benches and tables).

4 SÃO MIGUEL: LAGOA VERDE (map pages 52-53, photograph opposite)

🚌 bus to Sete Cidades: up to 50min on foot. Follow the notes for Walk 2 to the bridge that connects the shores of the twin lakes (20min), then see below.

🚗 car: no walking. Drive along the track on the western shore of the Lagoa Verde until it ends (1.9km).

Coming from Sete Cidades, take the track that forks right just before the bridge. It skirts the western shore of the 'Green Lake' (Lagoa Verde). There are many perfect picnic places under shady trees.

5 SÃO MIGUEL: LAGOA VERDE/VOLTA DO SALTO (map pages 52-53, photograph opposite) 🅿

🚌 bus to Sete Cidades: 35min on foot. Follow the notes for Walk 2 to the bridge that connects the shores of the twin lakes (20min); then see below.

🚗 car: no walking. Drive along the track on the eastern shore of the Lagoa Verde until it ends (0.8km).

Coming from Sete Cidades, a track forks off right beyond the bridge. It runs along the eastern shore of the Lagoa Verde (benches, tables, barbecues). Just before the track ends, you pass a well; here a path leads up some steps and over to a water-pumping house. Surrounded by lush vegetation, there are stone tables and benches on a small terrace (Volta do Salto) — a verdant and secluded place!

6 SÃO MIGUEL: PRAIA DO PÓPULO (refer to touring map)

🚌 Lagoa or Vila Franca bus; alight in São Roque — one stop beyond the church: 5min on foot. Continue along the road past the Hotel Barracuda for a few minutes; the beach is on your right. *continues*

View from the Parque Sete Fontes over São Jorge's highlands to Pico (Walk 16, near Picnic 18)

🚐 by car: no walking. Park in the large parking area above the beach, just east of São Roque.

*Lying between the villages of São Roque and Lagoa, this is one of the most pleasant beaches on São Miguel and stretches across several bays separated by low rock. There is **very little shade** however.*

7 SÃO MIGUEL: LAGOA DO FOGO (map page 61, photograph page 60)

🚐 only accessible by car: up to 20min on foot. Travelling north from Lagoa (Car tour 2), you will find a parking space/viewing platform some 1.5km beyond Pico da Barrosa, on the right-hand side of the road. From up here you enjoy good views over the Lagoa do Fogo ('Fire Lake'). The descent to the shore of the lake takes 20 minutes; a steep and narrow path leads down from the road. Take care; the firmly-trodden ground can be very slippery, and rainfall has created deep gulleys, so sturdy shoes are essential. Once down by the lake, you could continue left along the shore to the large pumice beach.

Lonely Fire Lake lies between precipitous mountain flanks at an altitude of about 570m/1800ft. The scenery is bleak and almost inhospitable, but is nevertheless strangely appealing. Even in summer it can be quite windy and chilly up here, so picnicking depends entirely on the weather and the clouds. Little shade — but you'll be glad to see the sun up here!

8 SÃO MIGUEL: CALDEIRAS DA RIBEIRA GRANDE (refer to touring map, photograph opposite) 🎍

🚐 only accessible by car: no walking. Follow Car tour 2 from Ribeira Grande. *The caldeiras form a small spa with a steaming thermal water basin and an old bath house from the early 1800s. Picturesque setting in a lush valley with a stream; some picnic tables with benches; ample shade.*

9 SÃO MIGUEL: LAGOA DAS FURNAS (map page 62) 🎍

🚌 bus to Furnas: 10min or more on foot. Get off the bus at the bus shelter near the end of the lake shore and follow the signposted left turn to 'Caldeiras'.
🚐 car: no walking. Drive from Vila Franca towards Furnas and take the signposted left turn to 'Caldeiras' near the end of the lake shore. The road runs along the northern shore past steaming rocks to the picnic area.

Furnas Lake lies calm and peaceful amidst wooded hills, but this impression is

Top: Baia da Praia, Santa Maria (Picnic 11); below: Caldeiras da Ribeira Grande, São Miguel (Picnic 8)

deceptive: on the northern shore you'll find percolating hot springs and mud cauldrons. The circular holes in the ground are used by the local people on the weekends as natural 'cookers'. Along the shore there are official picnic places under shady trees. In the summer you can even rent a boat.

10 SANTA MARIA: PARQUE FLORESTAL DAS FONTINHAS (map pages 66-67) ⊓

🚌 Santo Espírito bus from Vila do Porto (via Cruz dos Picos): no walking; the bus stops in front of the entrance to the picnic area.

🚗 by car: no walking. Drive to Cruz dos Picos, the road junction up on the central mountain ridge, and then turn south towards Santo Espírito. After about 0.5km you pass the Miradouro das Fontinhas on your right; the parking area at the 'Posto Florestal e Viveiro das Fontinhas' follows on the right-hand side of the road after another 0.75km.
This is a typical Azorean picnic area with tables, benches, fireplaces, and other facilities located in a shady wood. Nearby there is a small tree nursery (viveiro).

11 SANTA MARIA: BAIA DA PRAIA (map pages 66-67, photograph above)

🚗 only accessible by car: 9km from Vila do Porto; no walking. Drive to the crossroads in Almagreira and turn right to Praia.
*The Bay of Praia is the best sandy beach in all the Azores. There's a café and restaurant, but **little shade**.*

12 SANTA MARIA: BAIA DO SÃO LOURENÇO (pages 66-67, photo page 72)

🚗 only accessible by car: 14km from Vila do Porto; no walking. Drive to Cruz dos Picos, the road junction up on the central mountain ridge, and then bear north in the direction of Santa Bárbara. Ignore the left turn to Santa Bárbara and continue straight on; the road soon snakes its way down to the bay.
*The bay of São Lourenço lies in an ancient volcanic crater that opens out to the ocean like a natural amphitheatre. Its steep terraced slopes are covered by vineyards; the road along the bay is lined by summer houses. The bay has a long sandy beach punctuated by low rock, but **little shade**.*

13 TERCEIRA: MONTE BRASIL (town plan pages 78-79, photo pages 40-41) ⊓

🚗 by car (3.3km) or on foot (1h) from Angra. See Car tour 4 or Walk 11.
The wooded peninsula of Monte Brasil consists of four hilltops (picos) formed by the volcanic crater that shelters the Bay of Angra. On top of Pico das Cruzinhas there are picnic tables and benches, barbecues, and other facilities set in a shady wood. The lookout-point at the monument affords a magnificent view of Angra.

14 TERCEIRA: MATA DA SERRETA (map page 82) 🎍

🚌 Biscoitos bus; get off not far beyond the village of Serreta, at the bus stop 'Mata da Serreta': no walking. Note for your return journey: the bus departs here some 30min later than at Biscoitos.

🚗 by car (22km from Angra): no walking. Follow the coastal road via Serreta towards Biscoitos. Not far beyond Serreta the road runs through a wooded area, and the signposted picnic area comes up on the right-hand side of the road.

A large picnic area with all facilities, located in a dense wood. If you continue on the main road in the direction of Raminho, there is a signposted viewpoint on your left almost immediately, affording a fine view of the west coast.

15 GRACIOSA: TERMAS DO CARAPACHO (map pages 86-87) 🎍

🚌 bus to Carapacho: 5min on foot. From the bus stop, follow the village road eastwards down to the coast.

🚗 by car (17 km from Santa Cruz to Carapacho via Praia): no walking. The road to the spa turns off left at the beginning of Carapacho (where the main road curves right).

Carapacho lies on the lower slopes of the Caldeira, in the southeast of the island. At the eastern end of the hamlet there is a nostalgic spa down on the coast, set in front of steep cliffs. Nearby is a shaded picnic site with all facilities; down at the shore you can swim in a rock pool.

16 GRACIOSA: CALDEIRA (map page 86-87) 🎍

🚌 bus to Luz; get off at the bus stop 'Canada Longa': 30min on foot. Walk back on the main road for some 50m/yds, towards Praia, then take the signposted right turn to the Caldeira. Follow this road uphill, bearing left after some 500m/yds at a fork. The road runs through a tunnel (140m/yds long), to emerge inside the crater. Fork left not far beyond the tunnel exit on a road to the picnic area.

🚗 by car (17km from Santa Cruz): no walking. Drive to Canada Longa and follow the notes above.

An official site with all facilities in the wooded crater of the Caldeira. Shade.

17 GRACIOSA: MONTE D'AJUDA (no map, photograph page 20)

On foot (25min) from Santa Cruz. Follow the main street (Rua Marquês de Pombal) from the central square in Santa Cruz (near the twin pools) towards Praia, and immediately go ahead at a crossroads, on a small street with a yellow signpost, 'Sra da Ajuda'. Leave it when it bends left at house No 39, continuing

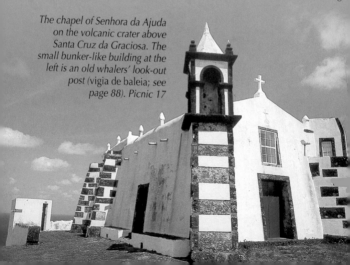

The chapel of Senhora da Ajuda on the volcanic crater above Santa Cruz da Graciosa. The small bunker-like building at the left is an old whalers' look-out post (vigia de baleia; see page 88). Picnic 17

ahead on the cobbled street (there is glazed tile, 'Caminho Velho do Monte d'Ajuda'). Immediately after the last house, turn left up an old footpath. Its old cobbles are still seen under the grass as you steeply climb the hill. Bear right at a fork, still climbing, to reach an old stone cross almost immediately. (Beyond it, the bullring in the crater basin can be seen.) Turn left at the cross and follow the cobbled footpath up to the chapel, Senhora da Ajuda.

Monte d'Ajuda stands sentry over Santa Cruz; its volcanic crater opens out to the town. There are three chapels on the crater rim. The oldest, Senhora da Ajuda, dates from the 16th century; just beside it there is an old whalers' look-out (see photograph opposite). Note the unusual stoup in the projecting section of the wall to the right of the entrance. Sit on the low stone wall to picnic, and enjoy the superb view out over Santa Cruz and its surroundings. **No shade.**

18 SÃO JORGE: PARQUE SETE FONTES (map pages 94-95, photo page 22) ⊓

🚐 (1h30min return on foot from Ponta de Rosais) or 🚌 (no walking): see Walk 16 (São Jorge 1), page 93.

The enchanting picnic area Sete Fontes ('Seven Springs') lies on the high-mountain region in the western part of the island. There are picnic tables and barbecues all around, in a varied wood with camellias, azaleas, splendid specimens of fern trees and other exotic plants.

19 SÃO JORGE: MORRO GRANDE (no map)

On foot from Velas: 30min. Head out of town towards the sports stadium and cross a pasture near a housing estate, to join a track that you can see ahead, winding its way up along the hillside. The track leads to the summit (Morro Grande), where there is a stone tower.

The cape of Morro Grande is a volcanic crater; its sheer outer slopes plunge down to the ocean. The hillsides are covered with shrubs, and the gentle dip inside the crater is cultivated. While there are no tables or benches here, the tranquillity makes for an ideal picnic setting. Some shade.

20 PICO: QUINTA DAS ROSAS (map pages 108-109, photo pages 110-111) ⊓

🚌 by car (3.4km) or on foot (1h) from Madalena. Head out of town towards São Roque, passing the old city hall. Take the right turn signposted to the Quinta das Rosas after some 800m. The road initially winds up between some houses and then climbs through a landscape with a myriad of stone walls, before reaching the entrance to the *quinta* and its gardens. Note: If you go to the *quinta* on foot, use the notes for Walk 22 (page 108) to return by a different route.

The Quinta das Rosas, formerly a manor, now belongs to the public. Its gardens have been lovingly laid out and display a wealth of different plants; some shrubs and trees are labelled. This is a pleasant place for a picnic; all facilities are available, including tables, benches, WC and drinking water. A stepped pyramid (photograph pages 110-111) serves as a viewing platform. Ample shade.

21 FAIAL: PRAIA DO ALMOXARIFE (map page 117)

🚐 bus to Praia do Almoxarife: no walking. The beach begins just a few paces from the bus stop.
🚌 by car: no walking. Leave Horta on the esplanade, heading north. Pass the 'Espalamaca' viewpoint before turning right down to Praia do Almoxarife.

The houses comprising the hamlet of Praia do Almoxarife are scattered over a wide valley that forms a long sandy bay where it meets the ocean. Behind the beach you will find the small centre, including the church, the bus stop and some restaurants. There's **no shade** *on the beach, but it has a wonderful view across the strait towards Pico. There are excellent facilities, including WC, showers and changing cubicle.*

Touring

Car tours are described for the three main islands of the archipelago, São Miguel, Terceira and Faial, giving you an overview of the varied landscapes and taking you to the main attractions. The notes are deliberately brief and concentrate on giving accurate driving instructions.

The **fold-out touring maps** (inside the back cover) are designed to be held out opposite the touring notes. A key to the **symbols** in the text is on the touring maps. Distances shown are *cumulative kilometres* from the starting point.

Take your time and don't plan too much for the day; driving is slow on the narrow and winding roads. Most of the main roads are in good condition, with an asphalt surface. The coastal roads mainly pass straight through almost endless roadside villages, where you should be *especially vigilant:* reduce your speed and be prepared for the unexpected.

The western coast of São Miguel, from the rim of the Sete Cidades crater. Notice the numerous small volcanic cones on the flanks of the caldeira. The lighthouse above Ponta da Ferraria can be seen in the distance, with Pico das Camarinhas to the right of it. (Walk 2, Car tour 1)

TOUR 1: WESTERN SÃO MIGUEL

Ponta Delgada • Pico do Carvão • Lagoas Empadas • Lagoa do Canário • Vista do Rei • Sete Cidades • Várzea • Mosteiros • Remédios • Capelas • Fajã de Cima • Fajã de Baixo • Ponta Delgada

85km/53mi; approximately 5 hours' driving; Exit A from Ponta Delgada (plan overleaf). The tour follows some gravel roads too.

En route: Picnics 1-5; Walks 1-3

Opening hours
Lagoas Empadas and Lagoa do Canário: May through September, weekdays 08.30-16.00, Saturday/Sunday/public holidays 10.00-18.00
Augusto Arruda Pineapple Plantation: June through September, daily 09.00-20.00, October through May, daily 09.00-18.00

On this tour you explore the huge crater of the Caldeira das Sete Cidades before heading down to the coast. Scattered along the coastline are idyllic hamlets where time seems to stand still. Near the end of the tour, you can have a closer look at a pineapple plantation where the delicious fruit is grown.

Leave Ponta Delgada in a westerly direction (Exit A). Passing the airport, you come to **Relva**. Turn right towards Sete Cidades just beyond the village. When you reach **Covoada** (8.5km), go straight ahead at the crossroads. Now you slowly ascend the western crater massif, the **Caldeira das Sete Cidades★**, but it's still some time before you get your first look into it! For now enjoy the marvellous view to your right over the low *pico*-zone — hilly country studded with numerous small volcanic craters *(picos)*, the result of the most recent eruptions. Cows graze on lush pastureland, and hydrangea hedges bright with violet blossoms run through the countryside — the whole setting glows with a wealth of colour. The white towers that come into view on the pastures are storehouses for animal fodder.

The road now approaches **Pico do Carvão** ('Carbon Peak'; 13.5km 📷). The slope by the roadside above a small quarry has been partly exposed by a landslide and shows quite impressively just how thin the fertile layer of soil on the volcanic rock actually is. A little bit further along you come to the **Miradouro do Carvão** (14km 📷). From here you have a fine view over the northeastern slopes of the Sete Cidades crater; small tree-lined valleys wind their way down to the coast through pastureland.

Soon an aqueduct comes into view on the right — once it was an important water supply. Just past this view, take the signposted left turn 'Lagoas Empadas' (15km; gate) and follow the gravel road uphill. Keep left at a fork and circle round one of the two crater lakes bearing the strange name **Lagoas Empadas** ('Pie Lakes'). Nestling between wooded slopes, these isolated lakes hide amidst the mountains. When you reach a roundabout by a small house (just in front of the second lake), take the first track to the left. Drive uphill past a gated left turn, until you reach the **Miradouro Pico do Paul** (16.5km 📷). This vantage point affords a magnificent view

out over more crater lakes sitting in the hollows of the surrounding volcanic cones at almost 800m/2600ft above sea level.

Return to the main road where you can once again see the old aqueduct and turn left to continue. Go straight ahead past a road turning off right after 1km. Shortly afterwards, take the signposted right turn 'Lagoa do Canário' (another gate) and follow the gravel road. Almost immediately, the **Lagoa do Canário** is seen down to the left between the trees; a flight of steps leads down to the shore of 'Canary Lake'. The gravel road quickly passes a picnic site (⛱WC) and continues to a signposted **Miradouro** (21km 📷). From here it's a 10-minute walk on a footpath to a spur affording a magnificent view down into the Sete Cidades crater — provided the clouds so common at this high altitude don't block your view!

Return the same way to the main road and turn right to continue. After 2.5km a road turns off right down into the valley of Sete Cidades, but first drive straight ahead to the viewpoint **Vista do Rei★** ('The King's View'; 26km 🏔 📷). From up here you can enjoy the famous panorama out over the Caldeira das Sete Cidades shown on page 20. The focal point of this landscape is a huge, almost circular volcanic crater with a diameter of some 4km/2.5mi. At the bottom of the basin, some 250m/825ft above sea level and enclosed by steep walls, there are two differently coloured lakes in the distance — the Lagoa Verde ('Green Lake') and the Lagoa Azul ('Blue Lake'). The sleepy village of Sete Cidades ('Seven Cities') lies peacefully on the western shore. Woods and pastureland around the crater contribute to the pastoral scenery, and there are some more, smaller lakes in the area — a most inviting area for walking, picnicking and swimming (Walks 2 and 3).

From the viewpoint drive back 1km to the turn-off left down into the valley of Sete Cidades. The road soon passes by the **Miradouro do Cerrado das Freiras** (30km 📷), from where you have another

Ponta
Delgada

PONTA DELGADA

1 Tourist information
2 Igreja matriz (Main church)
3 Post office
4 Market
5 Carlos Machado Museum
6 Theatre
7 Brewery
8 Tobacco factory
9 Sugar refinery
10 Hospital
11 Fort São Brás
12 Palácio da Conceição (Government buildings)
13 Court house
14 Town hall
15 Alfândega (Customs house)
16 Town gates
17 Igreja de São José
18 Convento da Esperança
19 Coliseum
20 Ermida do Desterro
21 Palácio de Santa Catarina
22 Ermida de Sant' Ana
23 Igreja do Colégio
24 Igreja de São Pedro
25 Ermida da Mãe de Deus
26 TAP, SATA
27 Football ground
28 Naval club
29 Old town

BUSES

All buses depart from the esplanade (Avenida Infante Dom Henrique), near the post office. The buses to Mosteiros, Sete Cidades and João Bom are on the north side of the road (near the Turismo), the buses to Ribeira Grande, Lagoa, Furnas, Povoação and Nordeste are diagonally opposite, on the south side (opposite the Alfândega, or customs house).

fine view onto the lakes. Shortly reach the **Miradouro da Lagoa de Santiago** on the left (30.5km ⏱), affording a beautiful view of the isolated crater lake hidden between wooded slopes. Continuing downhill, come to the bottom of the crater and cross the bridge between the Lagoa Verde and the Lagoa Azul (32km). Just before the bridge, a right turn would take you to Cerrado das Freiras (🚶P3), while a left turn would take you to Volta do Salto (🚶P5). Immediately beyond the bridge, a left turn would take you to along the western shore of the Lagoa Verde (P4).

Go straight ahead to reach the village of **Sete Cidades** (33.5km ✝✕). Leave your car here for a while and enjoy the harmony and tranquillity of this charming place. From the shore of the lake (🚶P2), your view stretches over the calm surface of the water to the green crater walls rising steeply in the background. You feel as if you are standing on the shores of an alpine lake, yet you are on an island in the middle of the ocean. Walk 2 begins in Sete Cidades.

From Sete Cidades the tour continues past the village church and through a quiet valley, onto the western rim of the crater. From these heights you look across pastureland and woods down to the sparkling blue of the ocean. Continue on the asphalt road to **Várzea**, where you meet the main road and turn right towards Mosteiros. After 500m take a wide turn-off left and go straight ahead at the crossroads that follows immediately. From **Ponta do Escalvado** ('Bare Point'; 40km 🚶⏱; Walk 1; see panel page 54) you look out over the cliffs along the west coast all the way to Mosteiros. The simple building next to the car park is an old whale-watching post (see panel page 88).

Return to the main road and continue towards Mosteiros. To get into the village, bear left at the next fork and drive down to the sea. **Mosteiros** (44km ✝▲✕🚆) lies on the coastal flats at the north-western tip of São Miguel. The magnificent coast with its frothing

PINEAPPLES: KING OF FRUITS — FRUIT OF KINGS

Cultivated under glass along the south coast of São Miguel, the pineapple (*Ananassa sativus*) came originally from South America and was brought to the island as an ornamental plant in the middle of the 19th century. The delicate fruit was soon appreciated by the wealthy; its cultivation in greenhouses started in 1864. The greenhouse glass is whitewashed, and the roof is pitched at a gradient of approximately 33 degrees.

Pineapple-growing has three distinct stages: in the *estufim*, or small nursery greenhouse, *brolhos* (shoots) are planted about 10cm/4in apart. They are well watered, and the temperature is gradually raised from 26°C to 38°C (79°F to 100°F) during the first four weeks. After six months, the plants are transplanted to the *estufas*, or larger greenhouses, where each plant is about 50-60cm/22in apart. Six months later they are transplanted for the last time.

Now it takes another 12-15 months, during which the fruit grows while the leaves are pruned once or twice. During the final ripening stage the crown of each fruit is also pruned.

About three to four months after the *estufa* is planted, the *fumo* begins. For about eight consecutive evenings, green leaves are burnt in containers placed along the paths in the greenhouses, so that a thick smoke is obtained. Next morning, the doors and skylights are opened for airing. This process, discovered by chance in 1874, is very important, as it causes all the plants to flower and fruit at the same time (due to the ethylene gas produced by burning acting as a phytohormone).

Pineapples were originally grown to supply the tables of the wealthy, and they are still an expensive delicacy. Don't miss this special treat when you are on the island!

surf (*P*1) makes an impressive contrast to the quiet and secluded lakeland district of Sete Cidades. Just by the village there is a small sandy beach where you can safely go into the water. Walk 1 sets out from Mosteiros.

From Mosteiros return the same way to the main road and turn left. Continue through an isolated region with pastures and woodland to **João Bom** (52km), where Walk 2 ends and Walk 3 begins. Immediately beyond a children's playground by the roadside, just before a small picnic area with pavilion (⩎), turn sharp left and head down Rua do Argentino. Almost immediately, turn right at the fork in the road in front of the Minimercado Pavão and continue along the village street.

Winding along the slopes, you gradually round the Caldeira das Sete Cidades. The roadside villages here in the northwestern part of the island belong to the Bretanha region (named for some Bretons that emigrated to this area in the 16th century). The next village en route is **Pilar** (54km ⌖). Continue along the village street for a short while, before curving right in front of a wooden grain store. An avenue lined by plane trees takes you back to the main road circling the island. Turn left to continue; soon there is a small chapel (*império*) dedicated to the Holy Ghost on the roadside to your right (see panel page 39).

Just past the signposted 'Grota da Levada' there is a picnic area (⩎) in a shady glen to the right. Soon take the signposted left turn to **Ramal da Ajuda**, heading down to the village church next to the bandstand (57.5km ♨). Turn right to continue along the village street. After just 1km, a beautiful windmill (📷) comes up on the left. It is built in the Flemish style, as was once typical of this region. Soon keep right at a fork, climb up to the main road and turn left.

A roadside viewpoint and picnic site on the left (59.5km ⇧📷 WC) affords a magnificent view out over the north coast. Soon pass the village church of **Remédios** (60km ♨), where Walk 3 ends. Continue along the winding road, mostly lined by shady plane trees. The **Miradouro de Santo António** (📷) gives you another beautiful view of the north coast. Tobacco is still grown in this area; the plant is easily recognised by its big bright-green leaves. In autumn the tobacco leaves are dried in high wooden racks that are seen in the countryside.

Go past Santa Bárbara and Santo António to reach **Capelas** (69.5km ☎), where you go straight ahead at the central crossroads. Then bear right at the fork some 150 metres further on (both forks are signposted to Ponta Delgada). Follow a village street uphill and keep left towards Ponta Delgada at the next fork (in front of a fountain). Past the last houses you reach the hilly *pico*-zone that lies between Ponta Delgada and the north coast. The landscape here is studded with numerous small volcanic craters and would almost look like the surface of the moon, were it not so intensely green.

Bear right at the next fork in the road (73.5km). Come to another fork after about 700 metres, signposted to Ponta Delgada in both directions, where you turn left. Soon you pass a huge parabolic aerial — a strange and futuristic sight in this crater landscape (75.5km). Bear right at the next fork (76.5km).

Soon reach the village of **Fajã de Cima**. Turn left at the cross-roads by the Cafe/Restaurante Os Soares (78km ✗; there is a school on the left) and follow Rua Nossa Senhora do Pilar all the way down to the beautiful village church of **Fajã de Baixo** (80km ♨). Turn left at the church on the street running to the right of the fountain in front of the church (Rua Jácome Correia), following a signpost for the 'Plantação de Ananás'. Pineapple plantations (see panel opposite), hidden behind tall walls, line both sides of this street. The **Augusto Arruda Pineapple Plantation** (81km M) is open to the public: the inconspicuous entrance to the estate is on the right, just before the road bends to the left — it's easily missed. There are pleasant, but neglected gardens surrounding the manor house. From the somewhat hidden terrace above the greenhouses there are good views (📷) over the plantations.

Return to the church of **Fajã de Baixo** and turn left down the village street (Rua Direita da Fajã). On meeting a road junction, turn right. After curving to the left, the road heads straight back to **Ponta Delgada** (85km).

TOUR 2: CENTRAL SÃO MIGUEL

Ponta Delgada • Lagoa • Pico da Barrosa • Lagoa do Fogo • Caldeira Velha • Ribeira Grande • Caldeiras da Ribeira Grande • Gorreana • Furnas • Vila Franca do Campo • Ponta Delgada

123km/76mi; approximately 6 hours' driving; Exit B from Ponta Delgada (plan pages 28-29). All roads are in quite good condition.

En route: Picnics 6-9; Walks 4, 5

Opening hours
Fábrica de Chá, Gorreana: Mondays through Saturdays 09.00-18.00. You will only be able to watch all stages of tea-processing from April through September, when the leaves are being picked. Tel/Fax: 296 442349
Museu Municipal, Vila Franca do Campo: daily (except Mondays) 09.30-17.30, Tel: 296 539100
Parque Terra Nostra, Furnas: daily 09.00-18.00
Museu do Presépio, Câmara Municipal, Lagoa: daily (except Sundays) 08.30-12.00 and 13.30-16.30; Tel: 296 912159
Museu de Tanoaria, Rua Dr Amorim Ferreira 5, Lagoa: daily 09.30-12.30 and 13.30-16.30
Casa de Cultura, Ribeira Grande: daily (except Sundays) 08.30-12.30 and 13.30-16.30

Note: If you want to enjoy a meal of *cozido das caldeiras* (stew) in Furnas, you should make a reservation in advance — for example in Tony's Restaurante, Largo do Teatro 5, Tel: 296 584290 or 296 584632.

This tour takes you to the historic towns of Ribeira Grande and Vila Franca with their beautiful squares and churches. Up in the mountains, you will glimpse mysterious 'Fire Lake'. And if you haven't already taken a morning shower, you can do so en route: you'll pass a hot waterfall splashing down an escarpment densely cloaked in lush vegetation, and the water isn't metered! You will also visit an old spa and a tea plantation. In Furnas, bubbling mud cauldrons and the famous park await exploration. There is much to see on this tour that an early start is recommended.

Leave Ponta Delgada by heading east (Exit B) along the coastal road to **São Roque** (3.5km ♣). Not far beyond the village church you pass one of the best sandy beaches on São Miguel, the **Praia do Pópulo** (4.5km ♠✕; *P*6). **Lagoa** (9km ♣♟✕M) has been the centre of the regional pottery industry since the 19th century. The clay comes from the neighbouring island of Santa Maria; the ingredients for the glaze are imported partly from the mainland. One of the potteries here welcomes visitors.

From Lagoa continue east on the main road before turning off left at 11km, following signposting for the Lagoa do Fogo. Bear right at the next fork (12.5km). Ignore the left turn to Remédios after some 100 metres, continuing ahead on the main road. Bear left towards the Lagoa do Fogo at the junction that follows almost immediately. The road winds up to the Serra de Água de Pau through bright green pastureland. The view becomes more breathtaking with every bend, and eventually the road passes close to **Pico da Barrosa** (947m/3106ft), a mountain crowned by a transmitter mast. You enjoy a fantastic panorama from the south to the north coast (19.5km 📷).

In the west the Caldeira das Sete Cidades can be seen, and in front of it lies the lowland plain between Ponta Delgada and Ribeira Grande, studded with numerous small craters.

Not far beyond the summit, there is a vantage point on the right, affording a first glimpse of the **Lagoa do Fogo** (📷; see panel page 60). Walk 4 takes you up to this isolated lake set amid precipitous mountain flanks. Further along the road, you can park in a layby (21.5km 📷) just before the road turns sharp left. From here, enjoy another fine view of 'Fire Lake'; you could even climb down to its shore (*P7*). But this is a bleak, somewhat inhospitable region, where clouds scud over the mountaintops, and a cold wind may be blowing … if so, continue straight on for Ribeira Grande.

As the road winds down the slopes, watch out after 4.8km for your left turn (signposted 'Caldeira Velha'). The road ends after 400m in a wooded glen, a scenic spot called **Caldeira Velha★**. In this idyllic setting, a hot (35°C/95°F) waterfall plummets down over an escarpment that is covered with lush plants and fern trees — a real paradise. The iron content of the water has stained the rocks a rusty red colour, which contrasts sharply with the intense green of the surrounding vegetation. On weekends, the locals gather here to enjoy a hot shower in subtropical surroundings, but if you come during the week you may well have it all to yourself. Just a short distance downstream, you will find bubbling hot-water and mud springs *(fumaroles)* along the stream.

Continue to drive downhill past a geothermal power station that uses the heat of the volcanic subsoil for generating energy. Then you leave the mountains, coming into pastures where black and white cows graze in the meadows. The slopes are partly covered by small woods and, behind the coast, the blue ocean shines brightly.

When you meet the main road at **Ribeira Grande★**, turn right into the centre (33km ♦✕🛒M). Start your walk through this historic town, which became a *vila* as early as 1507, at the bridge that leads across the eponymous river. From here, you enjoy a fine view out over the gorge, carefully landscaped with flower beds; in the background, another bridge spans the valley. On the northern side of the small municipal garden with its typical New Zealand Christmas trees is the town hall and, to the right, the imposing parish church. The baroque church of Espírito Santo, at the southeastern end of the municipal garden, has a richly-adorned façade of seashells. To reach the Museu Municipal/Casa da Cultura, follow Rua de Gonçalo Bezerre (opposite the theatre and the tourist information office), then turn right into Rua do Botelho. At the end of this street you come to a small chapel which is part of the museum.

Leave Ribeira Grande by heading east on the main road, then turn right (34.5km) on the road signposted to the Caldeiras da Ribeira Grande. A long cobbled avenue lined by plane trees takes you to the **Caldeiras★** (38.5km ✕⌂*P8*; photograph page 23), a small spa. The historic bathhouse dates back to the early 1800s.

Senhora da Paz, above Vila Franca

Now drive back to the main road and turn right to continue. At the next fork, pass to the right of Ribeirinha. Soon you come to the **Miradouro de Santa Iria** (48.5km 🚏📷), with a marvellous view of the north coast. The main road now winds high above the coast along the mountain slopes, opening up breathtaking views of the countryside. Numerous rivers run down to the ocean in small valleys, and the hills are densely wooded. A quick rain shower, perhaps … and then the sun breaks through the fast-moving clouds again. No doubt the tea bushes at **Gorreana★** (55.5km; photograph page 37) feel at home here on the humid north coast. The close-cropped tea bushes run in dense rows across the hills of the plantation. A turn on the left leads to the factory; its machines are mostly of English provenance. You can visit the factory and, before you leave, you can buy freshly-fermented green or black tea with its superb flowery flavour.

Not far beyond Gorreana the road forks (57.5km); head right towards Furnas, now climbing into the mountains. *(Car tour 3 continues to the left here.)* The surrounding countryside changes: you cross a secluded and undulating high-mountain region. Some 200m beyond a golf course, turn off right to the signposted **Miradouro do Pico do Ferro** ('Iron Mountain'; 66km 🚏📷), from where you have a magnificent vista over the Furnas basin. The Lagoa das Furnas ('Lake Furnas') is separated from the main valley by a low mountain ridge. Now drive back to the main road and turn right to continue the tour. Soon ignore a left turn signposted 'Salto do Cavalo' and wind down the hill into the Furnas Valley.

Be sure to allow ample time for your visit to **Furnas** (🚻🏨✕🅿), where Walk 5 begins and ends. Turn left at the T-junction in the village, then turn right in front of a public green space, following the one-way system. Reach the old bathhouse (72km), where there is ample parking. Turn left at the T-junction and left again to reach the **Caldeiras das Furnas★**. Clouds of steam reveal them from some distance. As peaceful as the basin appeared from the top of the mountain, it now reveals its restless volcanic nature: hot springs, bubbling mud cauldrons and small geysers testify to subterranean turmoil. Some rocks are so hot that the air above them shimmers. From a raised picnic area (🚏📷) you have a fine view out over the *caldeiras* and the river. For a tasty snack, don't miss the Furnas version of corn on the cob — maize freshly cooked in the *caldeiras*.

From the *caldeiras*, the village street takes you past the green space into the centre of Furnas, where a typical bandstand sits in front of the church. Turn right at the crossroads, towards Lagoa/Ponta Delgada. The street curves round to the left, leading to the western end of the village. The main road turns right in front of a building. Leave it here and continue straight on; then, almost immediately, take the first left turn, to the entrance to the **Parque Terra Nostra★** (❀; see page 64).

Return to the main road and turn left, soon leaving the village behind. The road winds uphill and approaches the shore of Lake Furnas. Watch for a sign to 'Caldeiras' and follow this road to the right along the shore of the lake. The placid lake at the **Caldeiras★** (76km ⌷WC; *P*9; Walk 5) lies amid steep wooded slopes; here, too, the ground boils and bubbles. Gases ooze from the lake, mud cauldrons open on the shore, and steam rises from hot rocks. Next to the picnic area, holes in the ground are used as natural ovens for cooking the *cozido das Caldeiras*, a stew that takes about three hours by using the natural heat.

Return to the main road and turn right. You follow the eastern shore of the lake before winding through woodland and pastures. Not far beyond **Ribeira Seca** you reach the edge of Vila Franca, where the Municipal Museum (of folklore; **M**) is on the left-hand side of the road. The music and pottery collections are especially good. Not far beyond the museum, take the narrow road to the right, signposted to the **Miradouro Senhora da Paz** (95.5km ✝⌷). This beautifully-situated hilltop chapel overlooks the whole Vila Franca area, surrounded by whitewashed pineapple glasshouses, banana plantations and sheltered orchards. Note, too, the typical tiles ('*azulejos*') decorating the steps, with motifs in blue on a white ground.

Then return to the main road and turn right. **Vila Franca do Campo★** (98km ✝⌷⌷⌷✕⌷) was the first capital of São Miguel. It was destroyed on 22 October 1522 by an earthquake and the subsequent flood of water and mud (after which the capital was relocated at Ponta Delgada). At least 5000 people were killed. Today nothing in this shady, sleepy village recalls its violent past. The central square, with its two churches and the town hall, is very picturesque. The gothic parish church of São Miguel boasts a wood-carved gilded high altar; the side walls are decorated with precious tiles (*azulejos*). Off the coast a small volcano, the Ilhéu da Vila Franca, opens out towards the village. Its sheltered crater is fine for swimming, and in the summer there are frequent ferries.

From Vila Franca continue on the main road along the south coast, which has a definite Mediterranean feel. Nor far beyond **Praia** (a part of Água de Alto; Walk 4) you pass the beautiful sandy beach of Praia (⌷). From the **Miradouro da Caloura** (104.5km ⌷ ⌷) you have a fine view out over the headland of Caloura. Now follow the coastal road through many settlements, through **Lagoa** and past Praia do Pópulo, straight back to **Ponta Delgada** (123km).

TOUR 3: EASTERN SÃO MIGUEL

Gorreana • Ribeira dos Caldeirões • Nordeste • Serra da Tronqueira • Povoação • Furnas

79km/49mi; approximately 4 hours' driving. The roads are generally in good condition. This tour can be combined with Car tour 2, but since this would be too long for one day, an overnight stay at Furnas is recommended.

En route: Walk 5

Opening hours
Fábrica de Queijo: not generally open to the public but, if you ask politely, a visit is usually possible on weekdays.
Museu do Nordeste, Rua Dona Maria do Rosário: Mondays through Saturdays 10.00-12.30 and 14.00-17.30; Tel: 296 488144

This tour will take you into the secluded eastern part of São Miguel. High above the sheer coastal cliffs, the road winds its way through green pastures and deep gorges. Beautifully-arranged picnic areas with magnificent views make good places to take a break. En route you may even be able to visit a cheese factory.

Approaching from the west, bear left at the fork not far beyond **Gorreana** (the 57.5km point on Car tour 2). High above the coast, the road twists through green pastureland. Pass through **Lombinha da Maia** and **Lomba da Maia** before crossing the green valley of the Ribeira Funda. Follow the main road past Ribeira Funda, ignoring the turn-off left to this village. The road runs in wide bends through two more valleys before reaching **Salga** (13.5km ✕). Continue ahead on the main road, ignoring the right turn to Salto do Cavalo.

Soon take the left turn to the **Miradouro Salto da Farinha** (🛋🎦WC). The road descends steeply to this magnificent viewpoint high above the cliffs. There is even a track winding down the gorge to the seashore, where a desolate pebble beach awaits the energetic. Continue on the main road and cross the green valley of the **Ribeira dos Caldeirões★** (20km 🎦), where a high waterfall plummets down over a rocky escarpment. Magnificent fern trees are scattered in the valley, and a channelled stream runs to an old watermill. The road continues to wind through verdant countryside. The slopes rise to the Planalto dos Graminhais, the 'Tableland of the Grasses', culminating at Pico da Vara (1103m/3618ft).

The **Miradouro da Despe-te Que Suas** (28km 🎦) affords a fantastic vista of sheer, almost perpendicular cliffs. Turn left at the crossroads in front of the church of **Santo António** (30.5km ✝). The road runs past **Nordestinho** to **Lomba da Fazenda** (36.5km ✝). Shortly beyond this village, a high bridge spans the gorge of the Ribeira do Guilherme, one of the rivers that never dry out. Once in the church square at **Nordeste** (40km ✝✕🖼M), ignore the turn-off left to the *'porto'* that comes up after 1km. The **Miradouro da Vista dos Barcos** (42.5km 🎦) affords a good view of the small fishing port of Nordeste.

The road now twists in a series of bends along the steep wooded flanks of the **Serra da Tronqueira**, sweeping through enormous gorges carved deeply into the mountains. Pass the **Miradouro Ponta**

Tea plantation at Gorreana

do Sossego ('Point of Rest'; 45.5km ⛩📷), then the **Miradouro Ponta da Madrugada** ('Point of Dawn'; 48.5km 📷) at the most easterly tip of the island. There is a sweeping view over imposing basalt cliffs three to four million years old, some of the oldest rock on the island. Slowly leaving this wild and remote region behind, you reach a more gentle landscape. Green pastures bordered by hydrangea hedgerows cover the rolling hills.

Ignore the turn-off left (55km) to Água Retorta. Just 1km past this junction, watch for the inconspicuous left turn *(not signposted)* to the **Fábrica de Queijo**. A visit to this cheese factory is very interesting, and you will certainly have an opportunity to sample the delicious product. The road continues to wind through lonely pastureland before reaching the **Miradouro do Pico Longo** on the right (61.5km 📷). There is a sweeping view over the wide basin of Povoação (literally 'Population'). The unusual settlement pattern of this town is easily seen from this vantage point: seven village streets radiate from the centre near the harbour, running inland on long ridges *(lombas)*.

After a short while you reach the **Miradouro do Por do Sol** on the left (63km ⛩📷). Ignore the left turn here to Faial da Terra. The road winds downhill to the centre of **Povoação** (68km ✝🍴🛒), where the first settlers on on the island came ashore in 1444. Of special interest are the chapel of Santa Bárbara dating back to the 15th century (the oldest on São Miguel) and the parish church (Matriz Velha) near the coast.

Past the village, the road ascends in bends and winds through wooded hills before descending into the valley of the Ribeira Quente ('Warm River'). Approaching Furnas from a distance, you can already see the steam rising from the *caldeiras*. Cross a bridge, turn right just beyond it and reach the **Caldeiras das Furnas★** almost immediately (79km ✝🏔🍴🛒; Walk 5; photograph page 63).

TOUR 4: TERCEIRA

Angra do Heroísmo • Monte Brasil • São Mateus • São Bartolomeu • Doze Ribeiras • Serra de Santa Bárbara • Furnas do Enxofre • Algar do Carvão • Pico de Altares • Biscoitos • Agualva • Serra do Cume • Angra do Heroísmo

112km/70mi; approximately 6 hours' driving. The tour begins in the centre of Angra at the Praça Velha (plan pages 78-79). Except for the Angra/Praia da Vitória dual carriageway, most of the roads are fairly rough and in poor condition.

En route: Picnic 13; Picnic 14 and Walk 12 are nearby

Opening hours
Algar do Carvão (cavern): irregular; enquire at the tourist information.
Museu do Vinho dos Biscoitos: 10.00-12.00 and 13.30-17.30 *(1 May to 30 September);* 10.00-12.00 and 13.30-16.00 *(1 October to 30 April);* closed Sundays. Tel/Fax: 295 908404
Casa Eco-Museu Dr Marcelino Moules, Cinco Ribeiras: weekdays 09.00-12.30 and by arrangement *(5 July to 13 August);* Tel: 295 907063, 907061 or 907169
Quinta do Martelo (Centro Etnográfico, Restaurante Tradicional): Tel: 295 642842, Fax: 295 642841

Start the tour at the Praça Velha, the central square in Angra do Heroísmo. Follow the main street (Rua da Sé) past the cathedral before turning left at the junction in front of the Azoria petrol station (this long square is called Alto das Covas) into a narrow side-street (Gançalo). Then take the second right (Largo da Boa Nova), leading to the impressive **Fortaleza de São Filipe/São João Baptista★**, the largest fortification ever built by Spain. Turn left just before the entrance to the barracks (guarded barrier) and keep right at the next fork (signposted 'Pico das Cruzinhas'). Follow the road uphill to the summit of **Monte Brasil**, the volcanic crater dominating Angra (3.5km ⊞P13). From the monument commemorating the island's discovery in 1432 there is a magnificent view (📷) of Angra.

Return to the petrol station and make a U-turn to head west out of town, leaving to the right of the petrol station on Rua de São Pedro. Keep on the coastal road, passing splendid manor houses; the Quinta do Martelo (**M**) signposted on the right can be visited. Reach the fishing village of **São Mateus** (10km ♨), popular with people from Angra who come here for a swim. Further along you pass Porto Negrito Beach. Not far beyond it, turn right inland for São Bartolomeu (11.5km; signposted). Bear left when the road forks almost immediately. Drive uphill through meadows and fields surrounded by stone walls to **São Bartolomeu** (14km ♨). Its church, *império* (see opposite) and *despensa* (pantry) form a harmonious ensemble in the village centre. The *despensa*, built in 1938, was a storage place for meat, bread and wine to be offered to the less fortunate. The *império* (1875) is one of the finest on Terceira.

Turn left and rejoin the coastal road at a small roundabout. Turn right to continue, going through **Cinco Ribeiras** (17km ♨ and **M** with domestic and agricultural utensils in an old farmstead which is more than 200 years old) and **Santa Bárbara** (19km ♨). **Doze Ribeiras** (22.5km ♨) suffered greatly in the 1980 earthquake — al

38

of its houses had to be rebuilt. Leave the coastal road by turning right on the road signposted 'Cabrito/ Pico da Bagacina' (24km). (Keeping straight on, you would come to Serreta: *P*14; Walk 12.) The road runs inland along the slopes of the Serra de Santa Bárbara; there are fine views to the right of villages along the coast.

Turn off left at 28.5km to the **Serra de Santa Bárbara**. Unless it's misty, this detour is extremely rewarding. The road winds across lush, green slopes up to the summit (1021m/ 3349ft) of Terceira's highest massif. There is a transmitter up here, and the look-out point affords a magnificent view over the island (34km 📷).

Return to the main road (40km) and turn left, soon passing a good viewpoint on the right (41km 📷). Having passed Lagoa da Falca (also called Lagoa das Patas; 43.5km 🍴), you reach the crossroads in the centre of the island (47km). First drive straight on, towards Cabrito. After 1.5km turn left on a gravel road to the **Furnas do Enxofre★**. Follow this road until it ends (49km) and explore the *fumaroles* — cracks and crevices in the ground giving off hot steam and sulphureous gases. Footpaths lead you through this strange and rugged landscape.

IMPÉRIOS AND THE ESPÍRITO SANTO TRADITION

Travelling around the Azores you will see small chapels, called *impérios* ('empire') in most villages. They are easily recognised by the symbols on their façades (see photograph page 126) — a crown, a sceptre and a white dove, emblem of the Holy Ghost (*Espírito Santo*).

These chapels are the focal points for the Holy Ghost Festival, a tradition that has never been officially approved by the Catholic Church. This charitable festival originally evolved in the Middle Ages and was brought to the islands in the 1400s by the first settlers; it still survives today. Starting on Whit Sunday, the festivities go on for many weeks. They are set up by a local group of men, a brotherhood, who organise the giving of food to the poor, the most important feature of the tradition. Fireworks signal the start of a procession from the church to the *império*. It is led by the elected *imperador* ('emperor'), a member of the brotherhood in charge of that day's festivities. Proudly wearing a silver crown with a dove on top, he has the great honour of guarding the crown and sceptre in his home until the next *imperador* takes over the reign. The procession is accompanied by the local brass marching band, or *filarmonica*, which plays an important role in village life.

After the procession, a beef soup called *sopa do Espírito Santo* is served, as well as *massa sovada*, loaves of slightly sweet bread made with yeast dough. Traditionally, the food is provided by the *imperador* who has made a promise to feed friends, family and the poor of the village, but sometimes money is also collected by the community to pay for the expenses.

Return to the main road and turn left. Bear left at the next fork in front of a monument dedicated to mountaineering, following signposting to the **Algar do Carvão★**. The asphalt road runs past a turn-off left and ends at a parking area (52km). Here a magnificent cavern lies inside the prominent crater cone in front of you. After your visit, return to the crossroads in the centre of the island (55km) and turn right on the road signposted to Altares/Biscoitos. There is a wild and ragged landscape all around you — the famous Terceiran fighting bulls are bred on these secluded pastures.

At the next turn-off left you can make another short detour, to the **Lagoa do Negro** (58km ⌨), a small lake at the edge of a wood. Then continue along the main road and almost immediately bear left at the fork for Altares, descending to the northern side of the island. Bear right at the fork in front of a farm with a silo crowned by a weathercock (63km). Pass the village sign for Altares and bear right at the next fork, to follow the Ribeira da Luz downhill. Down on the coast in front of you is the **Pico de Altares**, an old whalers' look-out post (see page 88), now an outstanding viewpoint (📷). The short climb to the top is well worthwhile. Park just where you meet the coastal road (65.5km) and walk along the road to the left for 75m/yds, until a field track turns off right (by a glazed tile 'Canada do Pico'); it takes you straight up the hill, crowned by a monument, in 15 minutes. Enjoy the beautiful view along the north coast and out over inland Terceira and its highest volcanic massifs: the Serra do Labaçal to the left (Pico Alto; 808m/2650ft) and the Serra de Santa Bárbara to the right (1021m/3350ft).

From the junction, continue east along the coastal road to Biscoitos. When you reach the village, turn left down to the **Porto de Pesca** (69.5km ✕). This bathing place is very popular with the local people: the black biscuit-lava rocks here (thus the name Biscoitos) form natural

Angra do Heroísmo, Terceira's charming capital, is under the protection of UNESCO's World Heritage list. Monte Brasil (Picnic 13) rises beside Angra Bay.

swimming pools. Return to the main road, turn left and continue through **Biscoitos** (✝🍽), past the *império* in the central square. The 'Agrícola Brum' (**M**), run by a family with a long tradition of viniculture, is on the corner of the first street to the right. All stages of wine-growing and production can be studied in the museum, prior to a wine-tasting. In the lava fields around Biscoitos, white wine made from Verdelho grapes is grown.

Continue on the coastal road through **Quatro Ribeiras** (76.5km) and meet a T-junction (82km): turn right for Agualva (literally 'Clear Water'). This roadside village runs parallel with the river, where there are still some partly-ruined watermills to be seen. Turn left at the church in **Agualva** (83km ✝) and turn right towards Angra at the next fork (86km). Pass a golf-course (88km) and keep straight on at the next crossroads; soon a dual carriageway carries you towards Angra. Turn left at the next exit (signposted to Praia/Serra do Cume), taking the second exit at the roundabout that follows almost immediately. Follow this cobbled road for a while, before bearing right on another road (94km), signposted to the **Serra do Cume**. From the top of this ridge (96.5km 📷), there are magnificent views to the west, out over typical Terceiran countryside with fields and meadows enclosed by numerous stone walls; the bay of Praia lies to the east.

Return to the dual carriageway and follow it back to **Angra** (112km).

TOUR 5: FAIAL

Horta • Castelo Branco • Varadouro • Ponta dos Capelinhos •
Norte Pequeno • Fajã • Praia do Norte • Caldeira • Flamengos •
Jardim Botânico • Horta

80km/50mi; approximately 4 hours' driving; exit A from Horta (plan opposite).
Most roads are in fairly good condition.

En route: Picnic 21; Walks 24, 25

Opening hours
Exposição do Vulcão dos Capelinhos: Tuesday through Saturday 10.00-12.00
and 14.00-17.00 *(1 October to 30 April)*; Tuesday through Saturday 09.30-
12.30 and 14.00-17.30, Sundays 14.00-17.30 *(2 May to 30 September);* Tel:
292 945165
Jardim Botânico at the Quinta de São Lourenço: Monday through Saturday
09.00-17.30 (summer only)

O n this tour you will visit the most westerly tip of Faial which
was totally reshaped by the devastating volcanic eruptions of
1957/58. A short detour takes you to a superb beach backed by
high cliffs. In the interior, you can peep into the huge Caldeira
crater. At the end of the tour, a small botanic garden, lovingly
landscaped, awaits your visit.

Head south along the esplanade in Horta. Soon leave the port
behind, following signposting for the airport through a new housing
estate. Join the main road (EN1-1a) and turn right, passing **Feteira**,
the airport and **Castelo Branco** (10km). Many houses in this village
were destroyed by the 1998 earthquake. Ignore the road off right
to the Caldeira (16km) and go straight on. When you reach an ivy-
clad manor house (Vila Maria), take the signposted left turn (18km)
down to **Varadouro**, a patch of summer holiday houses centred
around a small spa. Turn right at the junction in front of a fountain
(the old spa is 100m to the left) and reach a parking area (20.5km
✗WC). The rock pools on the black lava coast are most inviting for
a dip; there are showers and changing cubicles.

Return to the main road and turn left. Ignore the road off to the
right signposted to the Parque Florestal do Capelo (⊞). Coming to
a fork in **Cruzeiro**, part of Capelo (24.5km; Walk 25 ends here),
bear left for the Vulcão dos Capelinhos. Soon you pass the church
at **Capelo** and some houses. The landscape changes, becoming
increasingly desert-like as you approach the most westerly tip of
Faial — land that was completely altered by the eruption of the
Capelinhos volcano in 1957/58. There is a small museum on the
right-hand side of the road devoted to the eruption (27.5km **M** 'O
Exposição do Vulcão dos Capelinhos'; see panel page 44).

Soon reach a junction (27.5km) with a conifer in the middle,
where you turn left towards the Vulcão dos Capelinhos. Turn right
at the next fork. The road ends at the old lighthouse (28.5km 🕮).
There is an impressive panorama over the **Ponta dos Capelinhos★**,
a barren and inhospitable landscape shaped by the recent eruptions
— it's hard to imagine that, aeons ago, all the lush and green islands
of the Azores looked like this!

Return to the main road and turn left. Soon you pass through **Norte Pequeno** (31.5km ☗), another village that, like Capelo, was badly damaged by the earthquake. The landscape has been blanketed by a thick coating of volcanic ash and cinder. Keep straight on at the junction beyond the village (32.5km). The road now traverses woodland that covers a newer lava stream, the 'Zona do Mistério'. Take the signposted left turn (34km) down to **Fajã**. The narrow road runs down to some houses (✗) and continues to a magnificent sandy beach backed by steeply rising bluffs (36km WC,

HORTA

1 Tourist information
2 Praça do Infante
3 Igreja de São Francisco
4 Museum of Sacred Art (currently closed)
5 Assembleia Legislativa Regional
6 Igreja Matriz de São Salvador
7 Municipal museum
8 Post office
9 Praça da República
10 Market
11 Igreja de Conceição
12 Town hall
13 Police
14 Castelo de Santa Cruz
15 Boats to Pico
16 Fortified gate of Porto Pim
17 Observatory
18 Igreja de N S das Angústias
19 to Monte da Guia
20 Igreja de N S do Carmo

BUSES

Buses depart from the green space with the little pond, opposite the Marina. The buses to Cedros, Pedro Miguel and Praia do Almoxarife are on the side towards the city, the buses to Flamengos and Castelo Branco are directly on the esplanade along the harbour ('Paragem' sign).

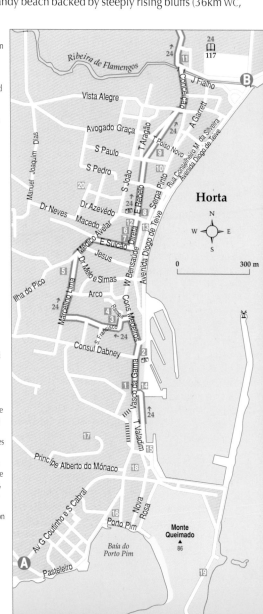

VULCÃO DOS CAPELINHOS

Created by a submarine eruption that began on September 27th, 1957, and lasted for an entire year, the bleak moonscape at the western tip of Faial is a vivid reminder of fierce volcanic activity. 'Rockets' of salty ash shot up more than 1000m/3300ft, powerful explosions occurred, and frequent tremors shook the whole island.

Ponta dos Capelinhos is at the very end of a straight line of volcanic cones that include Faial's Caldeira and can be traced over to the island of Pico as well. Relatively speaking, the volcanic centre seems to be moving west, so the eruption in this area did not come as a total surprise. Terrified residents of nearby villages had left their homes in time, so fortunately no lives were lost, but a thick layer of volcanic rock, sand and ash eventually buried the houses and fields. Some 300 houses were completely destroyed and almost every remaining house on the western part of Faial was damaged.

The eruptive activity of the Capelinhos volcano ended on October 24th, 1958, having given birth to new land covering 2.4 square kilometres. Some 2000 people had to be relocated; many islanders who had lost everything but their lives decided to emigrate.

The ruined lighthouse which once stood on the tip of the island bears testimony to the disaster: its ground floor is totally submerged in volcanic sand and ash.

showers). Here at the **Praia da Fajã★**, the surf is particularly strong and you can expect high waves most of the time — caution is advisable.

Return to the main road (38km) and turn left. Soon you reach the main coast road (EN1-1a; 39.5km), where you go left and through **Praia do Norte**. Shortly beyond the village (just before the bridge crossing the Ribeira das Cabras), there is a parking area on the left (41.5km 📷), with a glorious view out over the steep coastline down to Fajã.

Although the sign says 'Cedros', the next village en route is **Ribeira Funda** with its church (44km ✝). Leave the coastal road after less than 400m and fork right on the road turning inland, signposted to the Caldeira. This road climbs between hydrangea hedgerows and runs through gentle pastureland; the **Miradouro dos Cedros** affords a wonderful view over this landscape (48.5km 📷).

Ignore a left turn to Pedro Miguel and turn up right at the next road junction (54.5km) to reach the rim of the **Caldeira★** (60.5km 📷), where Walk 25 begins. From the parking area walk through the short tunnel to look out over the fantastic crater basin covered with cedars, junipers, ferns and mosses — an almost unreal landscape, rich in greenery. The summit on the southern rim, punctuated by a transmitter mast, is Cabeço Gordo, at 1043m/3421ft the highest elevation on Faial. Return to the last road junction and bear right towards Horta.

Baía da Ribeira das Cabras

Turn left at the crossroads at a chapel (69.5km). After some 0.6km turn right and wind downhill to the village church at **Flamengos** (73km ⚑). As the name suggests, Flamengos was founded by Flemish settlers. Unfortunately, it was badly damaged by the 1998 earthquake.

Turn right almost immediately, to cross a bridge over the river; then take the road to the left at the roundabout. Soon there is a parking area along the right-hand side of the road, near the inconspicuous entrance to the **Jardim Botânico** (74.5km ✿); this entrance comes up just *before* the driveway to the Quinta de São Lourenço. A visit to this small botanical garden is a good end to the tour. Many plants native to the Azores can be seen here, and the gardens have been lovingly landscaped. Continuing, turn left at the next road junction (at a church and an *império*; 75km). A bridge takes you across the Ribeira de Flamengos. Reach a crossroads where you continue ahead up a cobbled road (Walk 24 also follows this road). When the road swings left, turn right on the road signposted to the Praia do Almoxarife. Turn right at the next crossroad (straight ahead you would reach the beach; *P*21). Go straight ahead at the following crossroads.

The road runs on a ridge *(lomba)* that extends north of Horta; once it was crowned by numerous windmills. A wide valley extends to the left, opening up to the sea at the long sandy beach of Praia do Almoxarife. A viewpoint on the right (77km 📷) affords a magnificent vista of Horta. The roads runs straight down back to the esplanade in **Horta** (80km).

❀ Walking

Many of the walks described in this book run along tracks or old mule tracks through fields and forests; others follow little-used country lanes. Some of the best walking is along the old trails on Flores and São Jorge. These routes once connected the isolated villages before the modern motor roads were built. Please remember that the condition of the paths cannot always be compared with the well-maintained walking routes you might be accustomed to. Some paths can be very dusty in dry weather or quite muddy after rain, and they can even turn into small streams where they descend. So do reckon with landslides and deep gulleys caused by erosion.

Unfortunately, some of the lush vegetation that is so attractive on the Azores is also a menace. Two species that have been introduced to the archipelago, the Victorian laurel (*Pittosporum undulatum*) and the ginger lily (*Hedychium garderianum;* see page 13), are the greatest threat to little-used paths — as well as to all vegetation indigenous to the Azores. Both plants grow very rapidly, aggressively invading the landscape and soon creating impenetrable thickets, so that paths which are not kept open become overgrown within a few years. Beware of attempting to walk cross-country — the gentle appearance of the countryside is deceptive, and moss, brambles, deep gorges and thickets can make such a route either impassable or very hazardous.

Waymarking, maps

Only a few of the routes are **waymarked**, although in recent years some information boards for walkers have been set up. The **maps** printed with the walks are based on the latest official Portuguese topographical maps and have been annotated to show new roads, walking routes, and other information which should be helpful. Should you wish to 'have a go' on your own, you might like to purchase some of these maps. You will need ten sheets to cover the whole archipelago (scale 1:50,000; series M 7811). They are issued by the Instituto Geográfico e Cadastral. The Portuguese military maps of the islands (35 sheets; series M 889; scale 1:25,000) are even more detailed. These maps are *not available* on the Azores, but either set may be ordered from a specialist map supplier before you travel.

Weather

Pay particular attention to the weather. Do not undertake any walk in the mountains when you can see from the coast that the peaks are shrouded in clouds. In the summer, the cloud cover is hardly ever that low. Quite often, however, clouds develop *above* the mountaintops — then you can walk up into the mountains without worry. Since the weather tends to be changeable, you should always pay attention to the height of the lowest clouds; if they descend, do not continue your walk. The weather forecast shown on the local Azorean TV channel RTP is quite reliable and very helpful in planning the day. It is broadcast on weekdays at about 9pm, with an easily-deciphered weather map — you do not have to understand Portuguese.

What to take

Equip yourself properly for each walk, bearing in mind the distance and the height at which you will be walking. It can be quite cool high up in the mountains — easy to forget, when you are based in a hotel down on the coast. Due to the changeable weather, it is always a good idea to take **raingear** with you. **Waterproof clothing** that 'breathes' (such as Goretex) is best, since it reduces sweating. It is also important that you wear **sturdy walking shoes**, preferably walking boots with good grip and *ankle support*. Many walking routes are on loose soil or gravel, where you could easily lose your footing. A **telescopic walking stick** (or, better still, one for each hand!) will be a great help on rough terrain, especially since the gradients are often steep. They will increase your agility, ease the strain on your knees considerably and let you 'work' with the upper part of your body as well.

Take enough **food and water** with you on your walks, as well as emergency rations of high nutritional value, like chocolate, nuts and dried fruit. I would advise you *against drinking any spring water* (even where it flows into a basin); it might be contaminated. Take at least 1.5l/2.5pints of water with you on any walks over two hours.

Sufficient **sun protection** is important — the intensity of the sun can be very high, even if there is some cloud. In the summer,

View from the rim of the Caldeira das Sete Cidades towards Sapateiro (510m/ 1673ft), a volcanic cone on the west coast (Walk 2).

suncream (SPF12 upwards), a sunhat with wide brim and UV-protective sunglasses should always accompany you.

Below is the *minimum* recommended equipment for each walk (additional items are listed in the walk introduction as necessary):

walking boots	sunhat	compass
rucksack	sunglasses	torch
waterproof jacket	suncream	whistle
mobile phone	raingear	first-aid kit
light cardigan	bus timetables	picnic
telescopic walking stick	plastic ground sheet	water

Walkers' checklist
For your own safety, please remember:

- **At any time a walk may become unsafe**, perhaps because of a landslide after heavy rain. If the route is not as described in this book, and your way ahead is not secure, or mist closes in on a mountain walk, *do not attempt to go on.*
- **Never walk alone in remote areas**. If you are going to tackle a difficult walk, you should tell a responsible person (eg someone in your hotel or your taxi driver) exactly where you are going and at what time you plan to be back.
- **Do not overestimate your energy**.
- **Transport connections** at the end of a walk are vital. It is important to know when the last bus is leaving, in case you are delayed. A walk may take much longer than expected!
- **Be properly equipped** (see notes above).
- Please bear in mind that **twilight** is much shorter in these southern latitudes than in northern Europe. Night falls quite suddenly in the Azores.
- A **torch, whistle, compass** and **first-aid kit** weigh little, but could save your life.
- Finally, **do not take any risks** and do not walk cross-country through uncharted terrain or without a map on unknown paths.

Read the 'Important note' on page 2 and the Country code below, as well as guidelines on grade and equipment for each walk you plan to do.

Country code
Agriculture is the main source of employment for the Azorean people. Please remember that, although the landscape appears picturesque to us, for most people here life means hard work. People should be respected, as well as their land. Don't take anything from the gardens or fields. You can buy fruit and vegetables cheaply at the local markets or directly from the farmer.

Whale-watching has become very popular over the last few years and is being promoted as 'green' tourism. However, not all marine biologists are happy about whale-watching. While the warm and shallow waters off the Azores are visited by whales to produce their young, the increasing boat trips may disturb them.

These simple guidelines are obvious, but important:

- Help to protect the wildlife.
- Leave gates as you find them.
- Do not frighten animals.
- Walk quietly.
- Don't pick grapes or other fruit.
- Take all your litter away with you.
- Be friendly and polite.
- Do not take any risks.

Organisation of the walks

There are walks for all abilities in this book. Each walk begins with some basic planning information: distance/time, grade, special equipment and how to get there. Pay particular attention to the ascent. A total height gain of more than 500 metres/1600 feet is pretty tough going for the average walker. If the **grade** is beyond your scope, don't despair! There is often a short or alternative version of a walk, and in most cases these are less demanding.

When you are on your walk, you will find that the text begins with an introduction to the overall landscape and then quickly turns to a detailed description of the route itself. **The words *path, trail, track* and *road* have specific meanings in the walking notes.** *Path* means footpath, not usually wider than 0.6m/2ft. *Trail* is used for old routes, worn by time, for example cobbled trails. These are generally up to 2m/6ft wide. *Track* refers to an unsealed vehicle track, whether used by 4-wheel drives, farm vehicles or even motor cars. *Roads* are surfaced, for instance with cobbles or asphalt.

The **time checks** given at certain points always refer to the total walking time from the starting point of the walk, based on an average walking rate of 4km per hour and allowing an extra 15 minutes for each 100m/330ft of ascent. These time checks are not intended to pre-determine your own pace but are meant to be useful reference points. Please bear in mind that these times include only brief pauses where you might stop to recover breath or orientate yourself. A walk might easily take you twice as long if you allow ample time for protracted breaks — picnicking, photography and nature-watching. This is of particular importance regarding the last bus of the day or when pre-arranging with a taxi driver to be picked up at a certain time at the end of a walk.

Below is a key to the **symbols** on the walking maps:

expressway	21→ main walk and direction	⚑ ⊕	church.cemetery
primary road		⛟	car parking
secondary road	21→ alternative route	🚌	bus stop
motorable track	P picnic spot (see pages 20-25)	👓	best views
jeep track, etc		⚏	football pitch
old trail	⊼ picnic tables	⚙ ⌁	mill.windmill
footpath	↦ waterfall, source	⚓	lighthouse
—600— height (metres)	✕ ∩ quarry.cave	⚘	transmitter

WALK 1 (SÃO MIGUEL 1)

Mosteiros • Ponta do Escalvado • Ginetes • Rabo do Asno

Distance/time: 11.8km/7.3mi; 3h50min

Grade: moderate. A short, steep ascent at the start, then the walk undulates above the west coast. Ascents totalling 350m/1150ft **Note**: *the track after Lomba Grande is prone to landslides; you may have to make a detour on the main road.*

Equipment: see pages 47-48

How to get there: 🚌 from Ponta Delgada to Mosteiros; journey time about 1h
To return: 🚌 Mosteiros bus to Ponta Delgada; pick it up in Rabo do Asno (departures a little over 30min later than departures from Mosteiros).

Short walk: Mosteiros — Ginetes (7km/4.3mi; 2h20min). Easy, with a total ascent of 250m/820ft. Follow the main walk to Ginetes. Return with the same bus; departures in Ginetes a little over 20min later than from Mosteiros. You could also catch the bus at Socorro if you are pressed for time.

Alternative walk 1: João Bom — Rabo do Asno (14.9km/9.3mi; 4h40min). Grade and equipment as above; access by 🚌 from Ponta Delgada to João Bom. This route is ideal if you want to extend the walk or you have missed the early bus to Mosteiros. Walk down Rua do Argentino from the bus stop in João Bom. Turn left where the road swings right and go past the Minimercado Pavão, to follow the road straight through the hamlet; soon there is a chapel on your left. Beyond the last houses a track takes you down into a glen (Grota do Loural) with lush vegetation; there is a round cattle trough on your left (5min). Continue ahead when you reach the bend of a wider track 15 minutes later (20min). (This track rises to the left, to the main road.) Bear left downhill at a fork, soon passing a cattle trough. Pass the first houses of Lomba dos Homens and reach a wide junction of tracks with a cattle trough (on your left) and a fountain (35min). Continue ahead (to the left of the fountain) on Rua Direita do Pico de Mafra. The volcanic cone of Mafra rises to the right. After a few minutes, you reach two circular concrete shafts on the left, by some houses. Nearby is a beautiful viewpoint towards the strung-out hamlet of Pico de Mafra. Turn left down the footpath here, and follow the continuing village street past houses. Turn left at the T-junction in front of a chapel dedicated to the Holy Ghost (*império*); there is a fountain on your right (45min). Descend this street past more houses. Here, as in João Bom, you will see many traditional silos on stilts (50min). Reach a chapel on the right with a fine view down over Mosteiros (50min). Continue down the road, immediately passing a fountain with a cattle trough (dating from 1869). A few metres past it, the trail ascending from Mosteiros joins on the right. Now you have a choice: either make a detour to Mosteiros (1.2km/0.7mi; 35min return) or continue ahead, following the main walk from the 25min-point.

Alternative walk 2: Mosteiros — Ponta da Ferraria — Rabo do Asno (13.7km/8.5mi; 4h40min). Do the main walk, but make a detour to Ponta da Ferraria (adds 1.9km/1.2mi; 50min return; descent and corresponding ascent of 130m/425ft). Turn right into Rua Ilha Sabrina at the road junction in front of the first house of Fazendas. After a few minutes you reach a picnic place (some benches and a tap). Far below, almost down at sea level, you can see a rocky plateau called Ponta da Ferraria, with a pseudo-crater created by steam pressure — the most westerly tip of the island. The road winds down the steep bluff to the old thermal baths dating from 1888; there are hot springs in the sea.

This ideal starter walk runs high above São Miguel's steep west coast, affording marvellous views of the sea. The starting point is the village of Mosteiros ('Monasteries'), spread out on coastal flats and framed by steep bluffs. En route you cross rural countryside and visit idyllic hamlets, where time seems to stand still. Many traditional silos on stilts (*garnelos*) can still be seen — mainly to keep

50

hungry rodents away, but also because of the dampness. Bread was once baked in the huge ovens leaning against the old houses.

Start out at the CHURCH in **Mosteiros**. First follow the street which runs inland, to the left of the church. Pass the bandstand and a larger building inscribed 'Fundacão Brasileira 1863'. The row of houses ends in front of a high bluff; a glazed tile, 'RUA NOVA', is set on the wall at one of the last houses. From here climb the steep dusty trail that winds up the hill, and you will meet a CONCRETE ROAD (**25min**; *at this point Alternative walk 1 joins the main walk*). The walk continues to the right, but first turn left along the road for some 50m/yds, to reach a platform below a CHAPEL, from where you enjoy a magnificent view out over Mosteiros.

Now follow the concrete road south. The concrete surface ends almost immediately, when the road swings around a small gorge. Soon ignore the Canada de Pilatos off left and continue straight ahead, to reach the first houses of **Lomba Grande** (**40min**). Ignore also the right turn at a group of three plane trees and carry straight on. You join the surfaced road and keep on in the same direction, past a BUS SHELTER. Leave this road where it bends left in front of a CHAPEL (dating from 1914) and continue ahead on RUA DO CAMINHO VELHO (there is a tile on the wall). This track undulates through fields and pastures above the steep coast — mostly sunken and deeply cut into the easily-eroded layers of tuff and slag. Most fields are lined by giant reeds *(Arundo donax)* that serve as a windbreak.

Turn right at a crossroads for a short detour to **Ponta do Escalvado** ('Bare Point'; see panel page 54; **1h40min**), from where there is another spectacular view of Mosteiros and the rocky islets off the coast. The plain building by the parking place is an old whalers' look-out post (see panel page 88).

Return to the crossroads and turn right. After about 50m/yds you reach a junction. Bear right down the track, ignoring the road that ascends left to Várzea. Your track runs straight downhill and eventually skirts a volcanic cone on the right, the **Pico das Camarinhas**. Soon the track runs into an asphalt road. Some 80m/yds further on,

Coast at Mosteiros, with a derelict windmill (Picnic 1)

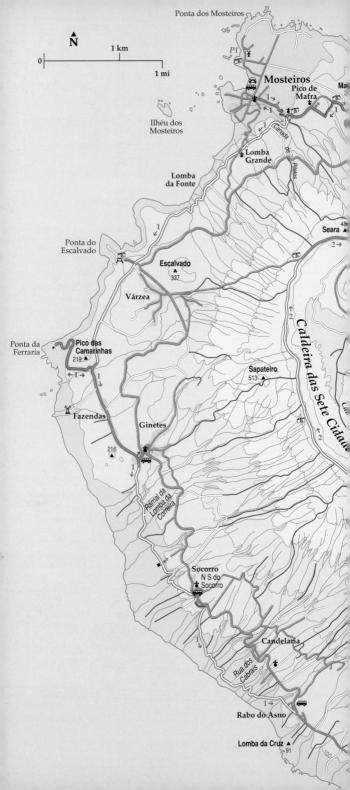

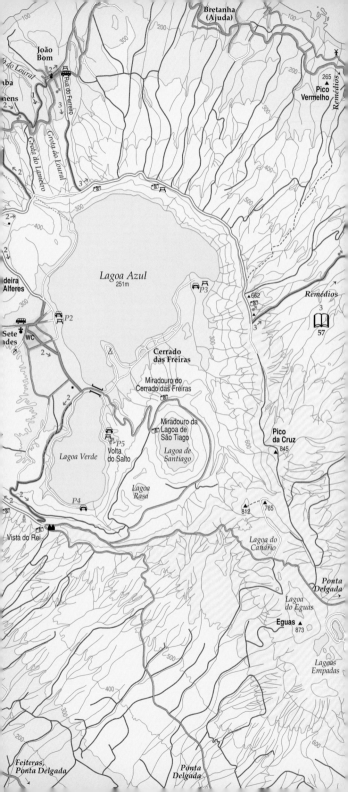

PONTA DO ESCALVADO

In 1811, a striking natural spectacle could be observed from this viewpoint. Preceded by four days of violent earthquakes, a submarine volcano erupted off the west coast. A new island was born on the morning of June 14th, when the eruption broke surface, accompanied by a thunderous din, great explosions, lightning and dark clouds of smoke and ash. Within eight days, the island reached a height of some 80m/250ft.

A British frigate, the 'Sabrina', was lying at anchor in Ponta Delgada at the time. The commander, Captain Tillard, had nothing better to do than disembark on the new island, where he hoisted the Union Jack on land still emitting steam and smoke. But this newborn member of the Commonwealth disintegrated rapidly and disappeared completely in October, leaving nothing behind but the name 'Sabrina' on some old maps.

just in front of the first house in Fazendas, reach a ROAD JUNCTION (**2h**). Before you continue through this village, you could make a detour to Ponta da Ferraria (*Alternative walk 2*).

Bear left at the road junction to follow the village street through strung-out **Fazendas** ('Country Estates'), where you'll notice huge bread ovens by some houses. Almost unnoticed, Fazendas runs into **Ginetes** (**2h20min**). At a road junction with a plane tree in the middle, bear right along RUA DO ALQUEIVE. (*But for the Short walk, turn left up the street to reach the church facing the village square with its bandstand and bar; the bus shelter is on the right-hand side of the main road.*)

The asphalt ends by the last houses, and a track leads downhill. Carry straight on along the main track, ignoring a track to the left ('Ramal da Lomba da Correira'). Soon bear left at a fork in a gully. Now climbing past two forks to the left, stay ahead on the main track. You pass an old COUNTRY ESTATE, the Casa do Monte, with an enclosed courtyard (**2h45min**); the Azorean flag was hoisted here for the first time in November 1897. There is an imposing fountain called Duas Bicas (dated 1816) on the left-hand side of the track and an old stone shelter for coaches beside it; the old stables are seen on the right almost immediately. A few minutes later the track forks; to your left is a telephone pole with a street lamp. Follow the track to the right, curving round a lush gorge and, about a minute later, fork left on the descending track.

Meet the main road in **Socorro** ('Help'; **3h**). There is a bus shelter to the left, with a flight of steps opposite climbing to the church, but turn right almost immediately, on a track descending in front of a wall with a glazed tile inscribed 'Canada do Socorro de Baixo'. Go about 50m/yds downhill, then bear left at a fork, still along the wall. Keep left until you enter a small gorge, and bear right where the track forks. Follow the main track to a WIDE FORK (**3h20min**), where you bear right again. Some six minutes later RUA DOS CABRAIS joins from the left; continue straight on. The track now leaves the coast and climbs to **Rabo do Asno** ('Donkey's Tail'; **3h50min**). Turn left on the main road in the village and follow it past a few houses, to the BUS SHELTER.

WALK 2 (SÃO MIGUEL 2)

Sete Cidades • Lagoa Verde • Vista do Rei • João Bom

See map pages 52-53 and photographs pages 20,26 and 47

Distance/time: 14km/8.7mi; 4h35min

Grade: moderate. A steep ascent over 350m/1150ft takes you onto the crater rim; the last part of the walk is a steep and sometimes slippery descent.

Equipment: see pages 47-48

How to get there: 🚐 from Ponta Delgada to Sete Cidades (journey time 1h); get off the bus at the church immediately on entering the village (the bus continues!).

To return: 🚐 from João Bom to Ponta Delgada

Short walks: see Picnics 2, 3, 4 and 5

Circular walk: Follow the main walk past the 3h-point, then take the first *major* right turn, to drop back down to Sete Cidades (11km/6.8mi; 3h30min).

Note: If you want to finish the walk in Mosteiros, turn left at the wide junction (3h50min-point) and follow Walk 1, Alternative walk 1 to Mosteiros.

The idyllic village of Sete Cidades lies on the shallow shore of the Lagoa Azul ('Blue Lake'), isolated from the outer world by the high walls of the crater. It's in a world of its own, where you easily forget that you are on an island in the middle of the Atlantic, and it almost feels as if you are beside a lake in the Alps!

The walk starts at the CHURCH in **Sete Cidades**. Follow the street past the village bandstand and the chapel dedicated to the Holy Ghost *(império)*, then turn into the first street to the left, just opposite the CASA DO POVO (there is a *minimercado* on the right-hand corner, which is not easily recognised from the outside). Follow this village street past traditional houses where big ovens for bread-baking, leaning against the houses, and silos on stilts, are still a common sight. There is a bakery (easily missed) in the house numbered 32; you can get oven-warm bread here — just ask for *'um pão pequeno'*. Go straight across a small intersection (there is a bar/restaurant to the left) but turn right when you reach a T-junction. Soon pass by a MANOR HOUSE with gardens and approach the BRIDGE which connects the shores of the twin lakes (**20min**).

Turn right on the track that begins between two small STONE PILLARS just *before* the bridge, on the western shore of the **Lagoa Verde**. It forks after some 80m/yds: the way to Picnic 4 is left, but the walk continues straight ahead, on the shady trail that rises between another pair of STONE PILLARS. Your steady ascent to the crater rim begins here. Japanese red cedars *(Cryptomeria japonica)* predominate in the forest. Bear left when the trail forks ten minutes later. The path is now somewhat overgrown, and you have to pass a landslide. When you meet a wide forest track, turn left, now climbing quite steeply to the crater rim. Ignore a MINOR TRACK off left (**1h 20min**; *this is the route of the Alternative walk after the detour to the Vista do Rei*).

Up on the rim, you come to a T-junction; the walk continues on the track to the right, but first turn left. Almost immediately you reach the **Vista do Rei** ('The King's View'; **1h40min**). Below you is the Lagoa Verde ('Green Lake'), further in the background lies the Lagoa Azul ('Blue Lake'), and along the edge of the *caldeira* smaller craters rise — a landscape of incredible beauty, tranquillity and harmony. Unfortunately, since 2002 the different colours of the lakes can no longer be seen, probably because of algae and pollution. And you will look in vain for 'seven cities' (Sete Cidades)! The viewpoint was given its name in 1901 when the Portuguese King Carlos I visited Sete Cidades.

Now head west on the track that runs along the rim of the crater. A few minutes later you pass a transmitter on your left. Further along you enjoy a spectacular panorama: on the left your view stretches across lush green meadows, wooded gorges, and the settlements near the coast all the way down to the Atlantic; on your right you look over Sete Cidades and the lakes. Follow the track beside the crater until you meet an ASPHALT ROAD after about an hour (**2h50min**; there is a viewing platform on the left). Turn right and follow the road for the next ten minutes. Then, just before the asphalt road makes a sharp bend to the right, turn left on a road that initially has an asphalt surface, but continues almost immediately as a GRAVEL TRACK (**3h**). Keep ahead on this main track past any turn-offs. Notice the beautifully-situated manor house on the hillock to your right.

The track forks in front of a distinct large BLUFF with engravings in its smooth tuff surface (**3h25min**). Turn left downhill to begin your descent. At times this sunken track descends between tall, almost vertical side-walls of tuff and slag. Eventually you cross the main road and continue down the road opposite. Soon you meet a wide junction at a CATTLE TROUGH (**3h50min**), where you turn right. *(However, if you want to finish the walk in Mosteiros, turn left at this junction; see Walk 1, Alternative walk 1.)*

Pass by the few houses of **Lomba dos Homens** and keep along the main track. Fork right some 25m/yds beyond a bend to the left (where there is another CATTLE TROUGH on the right; **4h05min**). Leave the main track three minutes later, when it turns right to the asphalt road: follow the track straight ahead, through some small glens.

Eventually the track comes into **João Bom** ('John the Good'). Walk straight on along the village street, past a chapel and a minor turn to the right, then meet the bend of an asphalt road (RUA DO ARGENTINO) near the Mini-mercado Pavão. Turn right uphill, to reach the MAIN ROAD almost immediately (**4h35min**). There is a children's playground to the right, and a small picnic area to the left. Opposite is a bar/café; the BUS STOP is next to it. (Don't be surprised when the bus heads off by going down into João Bom!)

WALK 3 (SÃO MIGUEL 3)

João Bom • Caldeira das Sete Cidades • Remédios

Map begins on pages 52-53
Distance/time: 9.8km/6.1mi; 3h50min

Grade: moderate. The first part of the walk is an ascent of 510m/1675ft overall, with a steep section at the outset. The last part is a descent of 490m/ 1610ft.

How to get there: 🚌 from Ponta Delgada to João Bom

To return: 🚌 João Bom bus to Ponta Delgada; catch it in Remédios, opposite the church (buses depart 20min after departing from João Bom).

Photograph: track along the rim of the steep Sete Cidades

Equipment: see the equipment list on pages 47-48

This walk takes you from the village of João Bom up to the northern rim of the Caldeira das Sete Cidades, where a magnificent panorama rewards you for the fairly strenuous ascent. You look over green pastureland onto the Atlantic and down into the crater of Sete Cidades.

The walk begins where the bus terminates in **João Bom** ('John the Good'). Here, at the corner where there is a small picnic area with a pavilion, the RUA DO ARGENTINO joins the main road. Follow the main road a few paces in the direction of Mosteiros, then turn left opposite the playground on RUA DO FERREIRO. This track runs between houses and soon leaves the village, climbing the hillside. Soon you pass a white WATER PUMPING-HOUSE ('CMPD 1975'). Keep straight on uphill at a junction. After a short while, ignore a turning left downhill and keep ascending. Bear right at the next fork (just past a left bend), now climbing quite steeply. Huffing and puffing, you eventually meet the track that runs along the RIM OF THE **Caldeira das Sete Cidades** (**1h**), where you turn left to continue.

Keep on this high-level track for a while, ignoring any left turns. From up here you enjoy really magnificent views. On the left you look over green pastureland onto the deep blue depths of the Atlantic; on the right you look down into the crater of Sete Cidades. Pass a sadly neglected LOOK-OUT POINT and picnic spot built in 1992 (**1h30min**) and continue on the high-level track, past further left turns, steadily gaining height.

About one hour past the look-out point you pass a TRIG POINT (a small stone marker) on your left, with the engraving 'IGC 1954' (**2h30min**). A gorgeous view now opens up to the east, stretching across the middle of the island with the *picos* zone, all the way to the

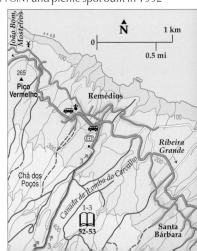

Barrosa massif. Ignore a turning to the left. A short while later, you reach a CATTLE TROUGH on your left, almost immediately followed by another TRIG POINT ('IGC 6'; **2h40min**). Your way down from the rim of the crater begins on the next track to the left. It is a sunken track in some sections, running rather steeply down the slope.

Pass a CATTLE-TROUGH on your left (**3h05min**) and continue to follow the main track, now referring to the map on page 57. On coming to a WIDE FORK (**3h25min**), follow the wide concreted track down left into a gully then up to a T-junction. Turn right downhill here. Then, at the junction in front of a small building, bear right downhill on cobbles. Passing the Remédios SPORTS FIELD/PLAYGROUND on Rua do Araújo, you meet the main road opposite the school (by a BUS SHELTER on the left). Turn left along the road to the CROSSROADS ABOVE THE VILLAGE CHURCH at **Remédios** (**3h50min**). There is a BUS SHELTER, a *minimercado* and a bar where you can relish a *galão* (milky coffee served in a glass), while waiting for your bus — which arrives on the opposite side of the road.

View over the Lagoa Azul from the crater rim. The small wood by the shore on the far side of the lake is the setting for Picnic 3.

WALK 4 (SÃO MIGUEL 4)

Água d'Alto • Lagoa do Fogo • Ribeira da Praia • Hotel Bahia Palace (Praia)

Distance/time: 13.5km/8.4mi; 5h

Grade: moderate-difficult. The route is straightforward, but the first part of the walk is an unremitting ascent of 620m/2035ft. The return takes you along a different route back down to the coast. Please take into account that the Lagoa do Fogo is often shrouded in mists; you should be prepared to be enveloped in cloud.

Equipment: see pages 47-48; optional: bathing things

How to get there: 🚌 Vila Franca, Furnas or Povoação bus from Ponta Delgada; get off a few minutes after passing the sandy beach of Praia, when you reach the second bus shelter of Água d'Alto; journey time about 1h. This bus stop comes up after the first bus shelter on the left-hand side of the road (by an electricity sub-station at the village sign for Água d'Alto).

To return: 🚌 Vila Franca or Furnas bus; pick it up on the main road, just opposite the entrance gate to the Hotel Bahia Palace (the bus stop is not marked). Departures are about 10min later than at Vila Franca, 45min later than at Furnas.

On this walk you will climb through gentle pastureland, dense woods and then the heather-zone, up into wild and almost bleak mountains by the southern shore of the Lagoa do Fogo. At 570m/1900ft above sea level, 'Fire Lake' is the highest lake on São Miguel. Swathes of mist scudding over the mountaintops and the shrieking of seagulls increase your impression of unreality. But all of a sudden the clouds break up and the crater lake, nestling between lush green slopes, shimmers in turquoise hues. Later you follow a water channel *(levada)* through woods and fields, to head down to the long sandy beach of Praia, for a dip in the sea.

Start out at the SECOND BUS SHELTER in **Água d'Alto**. Walk back a few paces from the bus shelter, cross to the opposite side of the main road, and head uphill on the concreted road that begins next to the BUS SHELTER (Caminho dos Escuteiros). It passes some houses and soon leads past a milk-collection building with an electricity pylon on the right, before going under the slim arch of a water pipe. The road climbs through undulating hills with fields and pastures. Bear left on the road at the fork in front of a CATTLE-TROUGH ('PPA 2-10-75'; **45min**) and walk gently downhill. Leave the road when it turns left downhill and climb straight ahead on a track. Bear right after 100m/yds, when the track forks. Soon you go through an IRON GATE (**55min**). Climb over it if it is closed; its purpose is to prevent vehicles from driving any further, but walkers have free access. Then continue straight ahead on the main track; there is a farm on your right.

The track runs along the right-hand side of the wooded valley of the **Ribeira da Praia**, and you cross a tributary on a BRIDGE (**1h 10min**). As you steadily wind your way uphill, the tall forest gives way to native scrub, where heather trees *(Erica azorica)* predominate. This area is called Mato dos Lagos — 'The Lakes' Scrubland'. Huffing and puffing, you eventually go through a WOODEN GATE and soon come upon a SHELTER carved into the rock to your right.

59

FIRE LAKE (LAGOA DO FOGO)

The irregularly-shaped basin filled out by the Lagoa do Fogo is actually the most recent *caldeira* on the island. It evolved in two phases some 30,000 and 12,000 years ago.

The last eruption began on 29 June 1563 after five days of violent earthquakes and underground rumbling. Great explosions produced volcanic ashes that were dispersed over the entire eastern part of the island, accompanied by brilliant flashes of

electric discharges. At night, the fierce glow reflected by the clouds could be seen from the islands of the central group — over 160km (100 miles) away!

Today the silent lake reveals nothing of its violent past. An early-warning system for earthquakes has now been installed on Pico da Barrosa.

Now the track runs through hills covered with grass, ferns and moss, an area which is aptly named Gaivotas ('Seagulls'), while slowly descending to the Lagoa do Fogo. The screaming of seagulls heralds the lake, which lies lonely and deserted; soon you get a first glimpse of it. Reaching a junction at the lowest part of the track, turn right on a minor grassy track (eroded in places) for a detour down to the deserted pumice shore of the **Lagoa do Fogo** (**2h50min**). The shore is only visible when the water level is low.

Return to the main track and turn right to continue uphill. Eventually the track leads down to a small WEATHER STATION (**3h10min**), at the point where there is a little building down by the shore of the lake. To the west, green slopes rise to the summit of Pico da Barrosa (947m/3106ft) which is crowned by a transmitter mast.

Walk down the gravel track into the valley of the **Ribeira da Praia**. In the upper reaches of this valley, the water of this river and its tributaries is collected and channelled in concrete chutes; small water pumping-houses are scattered all around. Further down the valley, all the water is collected in a small RESERVOIR (**3h30min**), from where it runs in an open canal *(levada)* to the right along the hillside. Following the path beside the *levada*, you contour along the wooded slopes of Pico da Praia.

Eventually you reach a BUILDING (**3h55min**) from where the water is piped down into the valley to feed a small hydroelectric power station. There is a sweeping view over green slopes to Vila Franca and the crater islet off the coast. Walk down the gravel track that begins at the building; it descends through pleasant woodland. Soon turn left downhill at a T-junction. There is a fragrant eucalyptus plantation covering the hillside. Ignore a track turning off sharp left and continue descending ahead. After a short while you pass a couple of old STONE HOUSES on the left (**4h15min**); continue ahead on the main track.

Ignoring several side tracks, you descend steadily until you reach a fork in front of a stone building; there is a CATTLE TROUGH to the right (**4h30min**). Bear left on the field track here; there is a fine view over fields and pastures. Bear right downhill when you meet an asphalt road. Now descend steadily; soon there is a view to the left down into the gorge of the Ribeira da Praia. You pass by some partially-abandoned houses before joining the main road. Turn right, then walk down a path past the **Hotel Bahia Palace** to the magnificent SANDY BEACH of **Praia** (**5h**), where there is a beach bar (showers and WC) with a beautiful sea view. *Wave down* the bus just in front of the ENTRANCE GATE to the hotel.

WALK 5 (SÃO MIGUEL 5)

Furnas • Lagoa das Furnas • Parque Terra Nostra • Caldeiras das Furnas • Furnas

Distance/time: 11km/6.8mi; 3h20min (allow up to two hours to visit the park, including bathing)

Grade: moderate, with an easy overall climb of 80m/260ft

Equipment: see pages 47-48; optional: bathing things

How to get there: 🚌 from Ponta Delgada to Furnas via Ribeira Grande (northern line) or 🚌 from Ponta Delgada to Povoação via Furnas (southern line); alight from the bus in Furnas at the bus stop in front of the entrance to the Parque Terra Nostra (there is a bus shelter dated 1994). Journey time approximately 1h30min
To return: 🚌 from Furnas to Ponta Delgada via Ribeira Grande (northern line) or 🚌 from Povoação to Ponta Delgada via Furnas (southern line); pick up the bus at the same stop in Furnas. The bus from Povoação departs Furnas about 25min later than the bus from Ribeira Grande.

Opening hours
Parque Terra Nostra: daily 09.00-18.00

Encircled by high forest-covered slopes, the picturesque village of Furnas lies scattered in a wide green basin. Fruit and vegetables are grown in the fertile gardens around the village, cows graze on the lush pastures, and the sound of cowbells can be heard from far off … you could be forgiven for thinking that you were in Switzerland. But this peaceful countryside is of volcanic origin — just like the rest of the island — and nowhere on São Miguel is this more obvious than here. With its hot springs, boiling mud cauldrons and steam clouds, Furnas seems to open up into the centre of the earth. Above the village, hidden behind a small mountain ridge, lies tranquil Furnas Lake. But beneath its surface the earth also boils and bubbles, and along the shore there are more mud cauldrons and hot rocks.

Start the walk at the bus stop and road junction (Largo Marques

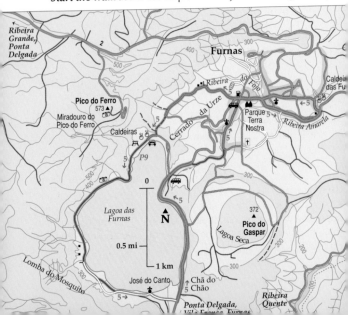

The Caldeiras das Furnas, where it boils and bubbles everywhere

da Praia e Monfort) in front of the entrance to the **Parque Terra Nostra** in **Furnas**. With your back to the park entrance, follow the main road briefly to the right, then turn left opposite a tiled wall plaque depicting a map of the island. Pass a PETROL STATION immediately and leave the main road where it bends to the left; continue straight ahead on a lane climbing between houses (Canada do Ferreiro).

Having left the last houses behind, you find yourself amidst rolling fields and pastures framed by steep escarpments. Stay on the road and walk straight on past some small buildings on your right. The surrounding area is called Cerrado da Urze — 'Heather Tree Enclosure'. Leave the road 10 minutes later, where it makes a broad sweep to the left, going straight ahead on a track. This climbs ever more steeply up a small wooded mountain ridge. Furnas Lake lies hidden behind it. At the top of the rise, turn left downhill. Soon you get a whiff of sulphur, as you pass by hot, steaming rocks and reach the northern shore of the **Lagoa das Furnas**.

Turn right on the road along the shore to reach the mud and hot water springs *(fumaroles)*, called **Caldeiras** locally (**45min**) — their steam clouds make them visible from quite a long way off. On weekends the locals use the holes in the ground here as natural 'cookers' for the preparation of their *cozido*. Should you be tempted to try making this stew of beef, vegetables and potatoes yourself, remember that it takes several hours to cook!

Cross the shallow stream behind the PICNIC AREA (Picnic 9) and continue on the track (closed to vehicles) that skirts the western side of the lake at the foot of wooded escarpments. Near a private estate, the track leads through a dense BAMBOO GROVE (**1h30min**). Keep following the gravel track around the southern shore of the lake. Old villas (some of which are abandoned) stand in enchanting gardens, hidden between Norfolk pines, fern trees, dragon trees and other exotic plants. At this peaceful spot, you can easily forget the volcanic turbulence nearby — and underneath you!

Bear left at a fork, to follow the track closest to the shore, soon rejoining the main track. You pass the chapel **José do Canto** (**1h50min**) and soon meet the cobbled main road. Turn left and follow the road skirting the lake. Ignore the left turn to the *caldeiras* opposite a BUS SHELTER (**2h20min**) and continue ahead on the main road, now leaving the lake behind. Ignore two consecutive turns on your right (both gated) almost immediately, but bear right down-

PARQUE TERRA NOSTRA

This enchanting park was originally founded by Thomas Hickling, the American Vice-Consul to the Azores.

In 1780 he built a simple summer house (the so-called 'Yankee Hall') on the site where the Casa do Parque stands today, and had trees from his homeland planted around it.

The estate was acquired in 1848 by the noble da Praia family, who extended the park and reshaped it; in those years it was laid out in the style of an English garden.

In the 1930s the Bensaude family took over the estate and subsequently built the Hotel Terra Nostra. They extended the park to its present 12.5ha (30 acres) and opened it to the public.

Thanks to the warm and humid climate, splendid fern trees, camellias, palm ferns (*cycas*) and many other exotic plants from around the world flourish here. There's another speciality in the park — a thermal swimming pool with murky yellow water — more inviting than it looks!

hill on an asphalt road a few minutes later. It leads through a lush valley and approaches **Furnas**.

Pass the first houses and join a village street (RUA ÁGUA QUENTE); follow it straight ahead. Soon you cross the **Ribeira Amarela** ('Yellow Stream'), a rusty brook coloured by iron oxides, and pass by a small CHURCH. Then you arrive back at the bus shelter opposite the entrance to the **Parque Terra Nostra (2h40min)**. Turn right to visit the park.

Leave the park again through the main gate and follow the street to the right, back to the corner opposite the tiled island map. Continue ahead for a few paces, before turning right at a fountain into RUA JOSÉ JACINTO BOTELHO, soon passing the Hotel Terra Nostra. Cross a bridge over the **Ribeira do Fojo** ('Stream of the Cave') and bear right on AVENIDA DR MANUEL ARRIAGA at the road junction just beyond the stream. This brings you to the nostalgic spa. Beyond the spa a road turns left uphill to the **Caldeiras das Furnas (3h05min)**. Here it boils and bubbles everywhere; dense clouds of steam rise from the *fumaroles*. There are stalls where you can get hot corn on the cob, freshly cooked in the *caldeiras* — a real treat!

Follow the village street straight past houses and a public garden. Then, when you reach a road junction near the village church, walk almost straight ahead on RUA MARIA EUGENIA MONIZ OLIVEIRA. Recross the Ribeira do Fojo and pass the Hotel Terra Nostra again, before turning left, back to the BUS STOP opposite the entrance to the **Parque Terra Nostra** in **Furnas (3h20min)**. The bus first *passes*, then returns a couple of minutes later, stopping opposite the shelter.

WALK 6 (SANTA MARIA 1)

Paul de Baixo • Paul de Cima • Barreiro Faneco • Chã de João Tomé • Parque Florestal • Ribeira do Engenho • Paul de Baixo

Distance/time: 10.9km/6.8mi; 3h 30min

Grade: easy. The route is almost level walking and follows tracks and asphalt roads. Overall ascent of 310m/1015ft

Equipment: see pages 47-48

How to get there and return: 🚌 or 🚗 to Paul de Baixo; get off at the bus shelter not far past the village sign or park your car here.

Shorter walk: Circular walk omitting the detour to the Parque Florestal (8km; 2h25min). Easy, with an overall ascent of 170m/560ft; access/ equipment as above. Follow the main walk to the 1h10min-point and turn left along the main road for a few paces, then fork sharp right on the village street. Now follow the notes from the 2h15min-point.

Alternative walk: Paul de Baixo — Parque Florestal — Pico Alto — Cruz dos Picos (8.9km/5.5mi; 3h30min). Strenuous, with a long steep ascent totalling 480m/1575ft. Some sections of woodland path are badly overgrown. Access/equipment as above, return by 🚌 from Cruz dos Picos. Follow the main walk to the two old forestry houses (1h50min) and go past the front of the buildings over the grassy clearing. Beyond the second forestry house you pass a ruined WC, after which you ascend a woodland path that is overgrown in places. This path winds its way steadily uphill through thick woodland before running along the crest of the island's central mountain ridge; thanks to the dense vegetation it is not vertiginous. When the path begins to descend slightly, you reach a distinct fork by Pico da Faleira; bear right here (2h30min). Soon you pass a concrete shelter on the left. Continue on the old ridge path; it's hard going in places because of fallen trees and ginger lily running wild. The path joins a small road at Pico Alto (2h55min). On the opposite side of the road, slightly to your right, take steps up to the summit of Pico Alto (587m/1925ft; 3h), crowned by NATO and civil air control transmitter masts. When you've soaked up the brilliant panorama from this highest point on the island, step back down to the road and follow it to the right through a cutting in the rock, descending steadily through woodland. Meet a T-junction and turn left for 150m/yds, to a crossroads (Cruz dos Picos; 3h30min). There is a bus shelter in the middle of the junction.

Photograph: Barreiro Faneco

T his walk leads from the grasslands of the flat western part of Santa Maria, barren and parched in summer but lush and green in winter, towards the wooded mountain ridge rising in the middle of the island. All of a sudden you find yourself in the 'desert', a strange open plain almost bare of vegetation, its sandy soil glowing with intense yellows and reds. Clays crop out in different parts of Santa Maria. Near Vila do Porto and the airport, old clay pits *(barreiros)* can still be seen. The clay was once quarried and then delivered to São Miguel. This circular walk takes you to the wonderful natural woodlands on the slopes of Pico Alto.

Start out at the BUS SHELTER at **Paul de Baixo**, where the road to Anjos curves left. Facing in the direction of Anjos, turn right on the side-road and bear left when it forks after 100m/yds (to the right is your return route). When you reach the scattered houses of **Paul de**

Cima (5min), bear right at the fork. Soon the track leads through a small valley, crossing a stream with a FOUNTAIN on the right ('C 18-6-950'). Continue straight on along the main track, ignoring a track off to the left as well as a track off to the right that follows immediately (just after the main track bends to the right).

You pass by some houses on your left, grouped around the chapel **N S do Pilar (20min)**. The track continues ahead and passes a last house. Then you ignore a track off to the left, following the main track as it takes on a reddish surface and leads into a small 'desert' — the **Barreiro Faneco** ('Dried-out Clay Pit'). Continue on the clearly established track through the denuded area. Your route

gradually swings in a wide sweep to the left before you turn right at a WAYMARK POST near the end of the 'desert', to follow a clear track through the vegetation. Ascending slightly, the track runs through woodland and meets a T-junction, where you turn left on a gravel road. Pass through the lush green valley of the **Ribeira do Engenho** ('River where water is scooped up'; **1h**).

On meeting an asphalt road by a BUS SHELTER in the hamlet of **Chã de João Tomé** (**1h10min**), turn left for a short distance (past a couple of gravel tracks forking diagonally and sharply to the right). Leave the road where it bends left, by a stone plaque on the wall inscribed 'PARQUE FLORESTAL': turn right on a gravel track that runs

MATA-MOURAS
In olden days, during pirate raids, the inhabitants of Santa Maria used to hide their treasures in 'mata-mouras' — small holes in the ground, over which they placed stones. But these hiding places would not have been so obvious as they are in this photograph. More likely a hole would be dug in a field or pasture and a stone placed on top.

past some houses. Bear right on the main track by the last house. Keep following the main track as it gradually climbs through woodland. It ends at two disused forestry houses standing in a GRASSY CLEARING (**1h50min**). Here, amidst the dense evergreen woods of the **Parque Florestal da Mata do Alto**, you can enjoy a picnic in peaceful surroundings, listening to beautiful birdsong. What a contrast to the treeless lowlands and the small desert!

Return the same way down to the main road and turn left. Leave it again opposite the BUS SHELTER (**2h15min**), forking diagonally to the left on a gravel village street past houses. Rejoin the main road and turn left to continue. Shortly before reaching a bus shelter at the first houses of **Ribeira do Engenho** (**2h30min**), fork diagonally right down a side-road and cross the eponymous river on an old bridge. Soon rejoin the main road and turn right for a short distance before forking right on a gravel road at another BUS SHELTER. Pass the CEMETERY (**2h40min**) and follow the main track round to the right at the next junction. Pastures and small woods extend on either side of the track.

On meeting the GRAVEL ROAD again (**3h**), turn left A few minutes later, ignore a sharp turn-off left; pass a house and a minor track forking right immediately. After some 300m/yds (about five minutes later) you leave the gravel road, turning off right on a FIELD TRACK (**3h10min**). It climbs initially, running ahead between stone walls. All around you, stone walls divide rolling pastures with grazing cows and sheep; in winter, this landscape is surprisingly reminiscent of Ireland. Ahead of you, to the right, some air navigation transmitter masts can be seen in the distance. Continue to the left when you join the gravel road where the walk began, to return to the BUS SHELTER at **Paul de Baixo** (**3h30min**).

WALK 7 (SANTA MARIA 2)

Santa Bárbara • Norte • Lagos • Santa Bárbara
See map pages 66-67   **Distance/time**: 7.6km/4.7mi; 2h45min
Grade: moderate, with an overall ascent of 250m/820ft. Two muddy sections can be quite difficult to negotiate after rain, when they get waterlogged.
Equipment: see pages 47-48
How to get there and return: by 🚌 or 🚗 to/from the church of Santa Bárbara
Shorter walk: Circuit via Norte and Lagos (6.5km/4mi; 2h20min). Grade, equipment, access as above; overall ascent 190m/625ft. This route omits the initial section of the main walk. Diagonally opposite the school in Santa Bárbara, just in front of the central bus shelter, a gravel street turns off the main road at a fountain; follow it uphill. Leave it where it bends sharp right (it continues up to the cemetery); keep ahead on a track that is cobbled at the outset and runs through a cutting in the rock almost immediately. You come to a T-junction by a farm (20min); turn left and pick up the main walk at the 45min-point.

A circular walk that takes you into the northeastern part of Santa Maria, this ramble visits secluded countryside with scattered houses built in the traditional style — with window and door frames painted in white and blue and big chimneys. The decorative terracotta amphorae that can be seen in front of some houses were once used as cisterns for storing rain water. You set off from and return to the charming village of Santa Bárbara, nestling amidst gentle hollows on the lower slopes of Pico Alto. From here you walk to Norte, a scattered settlement with many abandoned houses. You return through a quiet valley on an old, rarely-used trail.

Start out at the central road junction next to the CHURCH in **Santa Bárbara**. Follow the main road towards São Lourenço/Santo Espírito for a few minutes. At the end of the right-hand bend, where the main road (now lined by plane trees) continues ahead, turn left up the steep gravel track. Pass a working SAWMILL; you can see two ruined windmills standing up to your right. When you meet an asphalt road (**25min**), turn left to continue. Just beyond the highest point in the road, fork left on a FIELD TRACK (**30min**). It runs high above the bay of São Lourenço, but the coastline is hidden from up here. Bear left along the main track when you reach a fork. Ignore a left turn just before a FARM (**45min**; *this is where the Shorter walk joins*). Soon meet a narrow tarred road, where you turn right.

This road rises initially. Soon you enjoy fine views to the left, out over the scattered houses of Santa Bárbara and the central mountain ridge rising in the background. Then the road begins to descend. At the lowest point in the road, just before it begins to rise again, fork diagonally right on a field track running towards a stone-built cowshed. Soon pass another cowshed on the right. Stay ahead on the trail which is muddy and waterlogged in places after rain. It runs as a sunken path in some sections and leads past two more sheds. Immediately after crossing a small STREAM, bear diagonally right on the main path when the route forks.

Turn left uphill when you meet a tarred road. Soon you reach a junction where you turn right on a gravel road. After a good

69

Houses at Norte; note the two distinctive styles of chimney.

100m/yds, fork left uphill on a minor track, to the chapel **N S de Lurdes (1h30min)**. From the terrace there is a good view of Norte's traditional houses. Walk back down to the gravel road and continue to the left. Pass the first lonely and deserted houses of the scattered settlement of **Norte**, in the isolated northeast of Santa Maria.

When the gravel road forks at a wide turning area, follow the track to the left between scattered houses, some of them abandoned. Soon turn right at a fork and follow the track downhill; a short section is concreted. Leave the track when it bends left and walk straight downhill on a path; a partly-ruined house with two chimneys stands to the left, and a stone hut with a tiled roof is up to the right. The path soon widens into a stony old trail, partly overgrown by grass and rarely used these days. It leads down into the valley of the Ribeira do Amaro. Further down the valley there is a wet and muddy section to be negotiated. A short time later you cross the bed of the **Ribeira do Amaro (2h**; dry in summer); there was once a bridge here, but only its low supports still remain. Follow the distinct trail up the far bank of the river, ascending the hillside. Bear left when it forks after a short while, just below a small house. The trail widens to a track and passes near the dilapidated old schoolhouse of **Lagos** on your right. The houses of this small settlement are scattered on the surrounding hillsides.

Continue to climb for a short time, before leaving the gravel road where it bends to the right **(2h10min)**. Go left downhill on a path that starts just by a PYLON (above a ruined house). Continue ahead on a contouring footpath almost immediately. It runs along the side of the valley of the **Ribeira de Santa Bárbara**. Eventually, the route bends left and back right, then crosses a stream and continues as a wide field track flanked by stone walls. Join the main road at a FOUNTAIN **(2h35min)** and continue ahead, back to **Santa Bárbara (2h 45min)**. There are benches in the small public garden opposite the BUS SHELTER, and a *minimercado* and café at the corner by the church.

WALK 8 (SANTA MARIA 3)

Santa Bárbara • Cruz dos Picos • Pico Alto • Fornos de Baixo • Santa Bárbara

See map pages 66-67   **Distance/time:** 10.1km/6.3mi; 3h45min

Grade: moderate. Initially there is a fairly steep ascent; the total height gain on this walk is 440m/1445ft.

Equipment: see pages 47-48

How to get there and return: by 🚐 or 🚌 to/from the church in Santa Bárbara

Short walk: Circuit around Santa Bárbara (4.8km/3mi; 1h35min). Easy, with an overall ascent of 140m/460ft; equipment and access as above. This short walk could also be combined with the main walk if you have enough energy. Start out at the church in the centre of Santa Bárbara. Standing in front of the main entrance, with your back to the church, cross the bridge and turn right. Immediately, bear right at the fork in front of the fountain. This track runs past the scattered houses of Boavista (its inhabitants truly enjoy a 'good view'), before climbing steeply as a sunken track, now with a concrete surface. Beyond the last house, the track continues between pastures. At a three-way junction (30min), turn sharp right, soon walking through a small wood. Beyond the wood the track begins to lead steadily downhill. When you join the main road, go left past the 'Feteiras de Santa Bárbara' village sign for about 100m/yds, before turning right just beyond the bus shelter (45min) on a gravel road. Passing occasional houses, the gravel road soon begins to lead down into the valley. Leave it at the end of a hairpin-bend to the left (1h), where there is a pylon on the right, forking sharp right down a path above a ruined house. Now follow Walk 7 from the 2h10min-point back to Santa Bárbara (1h35min).

This walk takes you from the friendly village of Santa Bárbara up to the highest summit on the island, Pico Alto (587m/1925ft). Enjoy a magnificent panorama across the wooded slopes of the mountain out over the whole of Santa Maria — there is lovely hill-country in the east and flat grasslands in the west. On your way back you pass through a wide valley to return to Santa Bárbara.

Start out at the CHURCH in **Santa Bárbara**. Standing in front of the main entrance, with your back to the church, head along the main track ascending diagonally to the left. Cross the STREAM and continue ahead, ignoring a turn-off to the right almost immediately.

Santa Maria landscape with typical wooden gate

Soon go straight ahead past another right turn at a CATTLE TROUGH ('CMVP 1966'). At a junction by a FOUNTAIN with another CATTLE TROUGH ('CM 1951'), bear left along the ascending track; it is concreted initially. At yet another FOUNTAIN you are leaving the last houses of Santa Bárbara behind, to climb an increasingly steep hill.

Reach a wide fork, where you keep left on the main track, now contouring along the hillside. On meeting an ASPHALT ROAD (**50min**), follow it to the right. You soon come to a major road junction, the **Cruz dos Picos** (**1h**), with a bus shelter in the middle. Turn right and walk along the road for 150m/yds, then turn right on a small asphalt road signposted for Pico Alto. It winds up through mixed woodland.

Soon after the road leads through a distinct cutting in the rock, you see an abandoned concrete building on the hillside to your left. Just before you reach it, climb some steps up to **Pico Alto** (587m/ 1925ft; **2h**) and enjoy the magnificent panorama from the highest peak on the island. It is crowned by NATO and civil air control transmitter masts. From here return the same way to the **Cruz dos Picos** (**2h30min**).

Continue straight ahead along the field track that has a gravel surface at the outset. It gradually descends between pastures and small woods. Turn left on meeting an asphalt road in the hamlet of **Fornos de Baixo** (**2h55min**). The road sweeps around the valley of the **Ribeira do Salto** ('Torrent') and climbs up the far side. At the top of the hill you meet a T-JUNCTION (**3h30min**), from where there is a beautiful view to the north over the houses of Santa Bárbara, scattered on the slopes in a gentle basin.

Follow the road briefly to the right, then turn left on a track that runs past some houses and a working SAWMILL; two ruined windmills are seen on the hill to your left. Then the track begins to descend steeply. On coming to the MAIN ROAD, continue to the right, to reach the centre of **Santa Bárbara** in a few minutes (**3h45min**).

São Lourenço Bay, east of Santa Bárbara

WALK 9 (SANTA MARIA 4)

Santo Espírito • Calheta • Glória • Cruz • Santo Espírito

See map pages 66-67   **Distance/time:** 11.6km/7.2mi; 3h50min

Grade: moderate. You follow field tracks and country lanes with modest climbs, with a total height gain of 320m/1050ft.

Equipment: see pages 47-48

How to get there and return: by 🚌 or 🚐 to/from the church in Santo Espírito

Short walk: Santo Espírito — Fonte do Jordão — Santo Espírito (7.2km/4.5mi; 2h20min). Easy, with an overall ascent of 170m/560ft; access and return as above. Follow the main walk to the Fonte do Jordão wash-house (1h50min) and turn right (instead of left). Soon, ignore the left turn to Malbusca/Praia and follow the road straight ahead through the valley of the Ribeira Grande back up to Santo Espírito, rejoining the main walk at the 3h25min-point.

Opening hours
Museu de Santa Maria: Tuesdays through Saturdays 10.00-12.00 and 14.00-17.00; closed Mondays and holidays.

This pleasant country walk gives you a taste of rural Santa Maria. It begins in Santo Espírito, a quiet village with a fine baroque church and an interesting museum dedicated to the history of the island, with household and farming utensils on display.

Start out at the CHURCH in **Santo Espírito**, with its imposing baroque façade. Follow the main road east past the church and immediately turn left at the junction, taking a side street that runs behind the church. Soon you reach the interesting museum of Santa Maria on the left; you can either visit it now or later. Beyond the last houses, continue ahead on a field track, descending through rolling pastures and woodland. Pass a house and cross a small BRIDGE, to join a TARRED COUNTRY LANE (**15min**) which you follow up to the right. A windmill comes into sight on the hill to the right.

Leave the country lane in a right-hand bend (just past a house) and turn left on a FIELD TRACK (**30min**). A peak with layered rock rises some distance ahead — the chimney of an old eroded volcano. Soon ignore a left turn and begin to climb. You are now passing the scattered houses of **Lapa de Cima**. Past the last house, the track runs downhill and enters woodland, where you bear left at a fork and continue to descend. Soon there is a section leading over an outcrop of reddish clay; *care is needed here* on the slippery surface. A short while later, you pass an ELECTRICITY POLE and the track runs below its cable. At this point, take a short detour by going down the path to the left. It crosses a channelled stream. Just on the far side, take the fork to the left and follow the stream bed to an open grassy area where there is an old HOUSE (**55min**) — an idyllic picnic spot. In February, the citrus tree will be bursting with oranges, but if you only taste *one* of the tempting fruits...

Return to the main route and continue downhill beside more electricity poles. Soon you'll notice some basalt columns on the embankment to the right — reminders of the island's volcanic past. Cross the valley of the **Ribeira Grande** ('Big River') on a bridge and climb the opposite bank. Meet an ASPHALT ROAD (**1h20min**) in the

73

View from the bell-tower of Santo Espírito's baroque church

hamlet of **Calheta** and follow it to the right; the window and door frames of these scattered houses are usually painted green. Most of the houses look well cared-for, but many are only holiday homes for emigrants returning to the island for a few weeks in the summer.

Pass the BUS SHELTER at **Terras do Raposo**; ahead of you there is a ruined windmill on the hill to the left. When you come to the old public wash-house (**Fonte do Jordão**; **1h50min**), the road bends to the right. Leave the road here: turn left on a gravel road. *(But for the Short walk, follow the road round to the right.)*

Just before reaching the first house on the left, fork right on a side-track that runs as a sunken track. The track widens as it leads through woodland and crosses a valley with lush vegetation. Meet a gravel road that is lined by lamp-posts and follow it up to the right. At a T-JUNCTION by some houses (**2h35min**), turn right on the main road. Leave it shortly beyond the highest point in the road, forking sharp left on a gravel track. Soon you pass a building dedicated to the Holy Ghost ('IRMANDADE DO ESPIRITO SANTO') and the church **N S da Glória** (**2h50min**). A short time later, the old schoolhouse of **Glória** is seen down on your right below the track.

Turn right at a T-junction and follow this track through the valley of the **Ribeira do Cachaço** before ascending on the far side. Meet an ASPHALT ROAD (**3h10min**) and follow it down to the right; the houses of **Cruz** are scattered all around. Leave the road where it curves to the left at a FOUNTAIN ('CM 1950') and continue ahead on a gravel track running between pastures and woods. On coming to another ASPHALT ROAD (**3h25min**), turn left. This runs through the valley of the **Ribeira Grande** and winds its way uphill on the far side, before leading into **Santo Espírito** (**3h50min**).

WALK 10 (SANTA MARIA 5)

Parque Florestal das Fontinhas • Fornos de Cima • Cruz de São Mor • Malbusca • Parque Florestal das Fontinhas

See map pages 66-67   Distance/time: 8.7km/5.4mi; 3h10min

Grade: moderate. You follow field tracks and country lanes with modest climbs, with a total height gain of 270m/885ft.

Equipment: see pages 47-48

How to get there and return: by 🚐 or 🚗 to/from the 'Posto Florestal e Viveiro das Fontinhas', 1.3km southeast of Cruz dos Picos (the main road junction up in the mountains on the road to Santo Espírito). The car park is on the right-hand side of the road, just opposite the picnic area (Parque Florestal). *Note*: Depending on how the buses run, you could also start or end the walk in Malbusca.

Small hamlets where time seems to stand still are passed on this walk. You explore the lovely undulating country in the interior of the island, where gentle green pastureland ribboned by hydrangea hedgerows alternates with shady woods.

Start out at the **Parque Florestal das Fontinhas**. Walk back along the road towards Cruz dos Picos; a tree nursery *(viveiro)* and two forestry houses are seen down to the right. Ignore a forestry track forking off sharp right. Emerge from the trees almost immediately, enjoying a nice view to the left over the western part of Santa Maria. Then turn right up a field track. At the top of the rise, the eastern half of São Miguel comes into view on the horizon when the weather is clear. Bear right on the main track at a fork, now beginning your descent.

Reach an old public WASHING PLACE in the small scattering of houses called **Fornos de Cima** (**30min**). Descend the tarred lane that begins here. Further down in the valley of the **Ribeira do Salto** ('Torrent'), you meet a T-junction. Turn right uphill, eventually passing the houses of **Cruz de São Mor**. Looking back, you have another good view (if it's a clear day) extending almost the whole length of the neighbouring island of São Miguel on the horizon.

Ignore a GRAVEL ROAD off left (**1h15min**) and meet the main CRUZ DOS PICOS/SANTO ESPIRITO ROAD (**1h30min**), where you turn right. After some 50m/yds, just beyond the BUS SHELTER, climb the gravel road to the right, cut deeply into the rock. Soon you bear left at a fork and continue to rise. A water-pumping house becomes visible up on the hill to the left. Soon you reach a fork: keep left on the main track. Not long after, you rejoin the main road and turn right to continue.

On the next right-hand bend, just before the road passes an old QUARRY on the right, go left downhill on a gravel track. Five minutes later, ignore two consecutive turns on your left, continuing ahead on the main track. After a few minutes, you reach the edge of an open MEADOW in a small valley (**1h45min**). A track turns left here, while the track running ahead briefly follows a hedge before swinging to the left on the far side of the valley. Turn left on the track in front of the meadow; you will return to this point after a

75

Willow-worker in Fornos de Cima

detour to Malbusca. Stay ahead on the main track as it runs through woodland and begins to descend. Some remains of old stone cobbles underfoot testify to the fact that this was once an important connecting trail.

Emerging from the trees, you find yourself in a small valley with fields and gardens. Meet the main road almost immediately and turn left for some 100m/yds, to the BUS SHELTER at **Malbusca** ('Hard Searching'; **2h**). The village takes its name from olden days, when the *urzela* plant, using for dyeing, was harvested on the dangerous coastal cliffs. Turn right for a short distance, then fork left opposite the old schoolhouse, just by a building with a tile inscribed 'IRMA-DADE ESPIRITO SANTO'. Go up to the small church of **N S da Piedade**, where you can pause on the terrace, enjoying the beautiful view. Scattered on lush hillsides, Malbusca's houses are all built in traditional style, with green window and door frames.

From the church continue on the track, soon rejoining the main road. (You could turn right here for about 300m/yds, to a mini-mercado where refreshments are available. It's on the right-hand side of the road, but is rather inconspicuous from the outside; some plastic chairs are in front of it.) But to continue the walk, follow the main road to the *left*, again passing the BUS SHELTER. Turn right after 100m/yds on the track you came down originally; it begins between a field on the left and a house up on the right.

Return the same way to the open MEADOW (the 1h45min-point of your outward route; **2h45min**) and turn left at the T-junction. Skirting a hedge, the track runs past the meadow and swings to the left on the far side of the valley. Leave the track when it bends to the left: turn right on an old footpath that climbs between pastures; some sections of it are badly eroded — at the outset, this path looks more like a river bed in a gulley. Ascending quite steeply, you eventually reach the main road. Turn left to follow it back to the **Parque Florestal das Fontinhas (3h10min)**.

WALK 11 (TERCEIRA 1)

A city walk through Angra

See also photograph pages 40-41
Distance/time: 6km/3.7mi; 3-4h
Grade: easy city walk with a climb up to Monte Brasil and some steps ascending to the obelisk
Equipment: sturdy shoes and adequate sun protection

Opening hours
Museu de Angra do Heroísmo, Ladeira de São Francisco: open Tue-Sat. *From 1 Oct-30 Apr:* 10.00-12.00, 14.00-17.00; *from 2 May to 30 Sep:* 09.30-12.30, 14.00-17.30 and also open Sundays from 14.00-17.30

How to get there and return: The walk begins at the Praça Velha, the central square, west of [2] on the town plan.

Photograph: many buildings in Angra have lovely wrought-iron balconies.

The history of Angra do Heroísmo dates back to the days of sail, when galleons crossing the North Atlantic dropped anchor in the Azores. As their main port, Angra soon gained enormous strategic importance, both militarily and commercially. During the late 15th and 16th centuries, mainly under Spanish rule, Angra was built as a city in accordance with the urban principles of the Renaissance, its streets laid out in a grid network. In 1983, just three years after a devastating earthquake, Angra's old town was included in UNESCO's World Heritage list.

Start out at the **Praça Velha**, the CENTRAL SQUARE in Angra. The imposing town hall, the **Paços do Concelho** [2] rises on the eastern side. Dating back to the 19th century, this fine building was modelled on the old town hall in Oporto. Inside is one of the largest halls in the whole of Portugal. Follow RUA DA SÉ westwards, then turn left into RUA DE SÃO JOÃO. This street is lined with beautiful houses and commercial buildings with splendid wrought-iron balconies. At the Hotel Beira Mar you reach the seafront (ESTRADA GASPAR CORTE REAL); follow it to the right past the old fish market, the **Mercado do Peixe** [3], now a restaurant. Angra's old shipyard was originally located in the small cove below the esplanade.

Shortly before reaching the **Clube Náutico** [4], climb steps up on your right through a large gate and turn left along the walls of the fort. Swing up to the right through the public garden (**Parque do Relvão**). Go through an old gate to meet a road, cross it and continue ahead on a cobbled road, gradually rising. Beyond a FOUNTAIN, you reach the imposing MAIN ENTRANCE [5] to the **Fortaleza de São Filipe/São João Baptista do Monte Brasil**. Note the coat of arms over the entrance gate. Construction began in 1592 during the reign of Philip II of Spain. Designed primarily to protect ships sailing to and from Spanish America, this fortress controlled the harbour of Angra. It covers the whole of Monte Brasil and is the largest Spanish fortification ever built.

Facing the main entrance, follow the wall to the left. Note the deep enclosures in the ditch, aimed at keeping attacking soldiers away. Steps lead down to an asphalt road which you follow up to

BUSES

All buses depart from the square south of the Palácio dos Capitães [11], where there is also a taxi rank. The Praia bus is opposite the post office [10]; the Biscoitos bus is at the entrance to the municipal gardens (Jardim Duque).

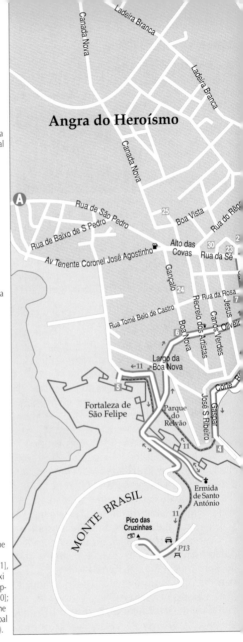

Angra do Heroísmo

the right. Go through a gate and bear left in front of the guarded barrier. The road forks almost immediately. Before you continue along the road rising to the right, you can take a short detour to the left to the Ermida de Santo António, past the old powder magazine seen down on the left. Then return and follow the road uphill. Leave it soon after it bends to the right, climbing a fairly steep woodland

78

path on your left. Join another road and turn right uphill. Turn right again at the road junction in the PICNIC AREA on **Monte Brasil** and climb to **Pico das Cruzinhas**. At the top, a column commemorates the discovery of the island in 1432; from the viewing platform there is a beautiful view of Angra.

Return the same way to the gate opposite the guarded barrier and continue ahead on the road (LARGO DA BOA NOVA). At the next crossroads, the **Hospital da Boa Nova** [6] stands on the left-hand corner. Supposedly the oldest of its kind in the world, this military hospital was built in 1615 by the Spaniards for treating soldiers stationed at the nearby fort. Continue ahead on RUA DA OLIVEIRA. Note the chapel dedicated to the Holy Ghost (rebuilt in 1916) on the left at the next crossroads; these chapels are called *impérios;* see page 39. The street runs straight ahead to a walled-in garden laid out on the steep hillside below you. Here you have a magnificent view of the marina and harbour (Porto das Pipas).

Turn left into CARREIRA DOS CAVALOS. At the next corner the **Antigo Paço Episcopal** (Old Bishop's Palace) is on the left [7], while the **Palácio Bettencourt** [8] stands on the right. Built at the end of the 17th century, this fine baroque palace now houses the Public Library and Archive. Step through the doorway with its beautifully-

79

carved masonry, to see the glazed tiles *(azulejos)* in the entrance hall and the staircase, as well as the beautiful wooden ceiling.

Opposite is the cathedral, the **Igreja do Santíssimo Salvador da Sé** [9]. It was badly damaged in the 1980 earthquake and a fire, but has been rebuilt. The apse is to the north, rather than to the east as is usual in medieval churches. In front of the cathedral you meet RUA DA SÉ; follow this main street of the city down to the right. Then turn left into RUA DO PALÁCIO and fork right at the POST OFFICE [10]. The imposing church of the former Jesuits' convent rises above a great flight of steps. The richly-decorated interior holds some treasures, including gilded wood-carvings, Delft tiles and a wooden ceiling. Unfortunately the church is only open during mass. The former monastic complex was turned into a palace in 1776 to accommodate the Major General of the Azores — hence its name, **Palácio dos Capitães Generais** [11]; today it houses government departments. Go past the church into the well-planted municipal garden, **Jardim Duque da Terceira**.

Climb the steps at the far left-hand end of the garden to **Outeiro da Memória** ('Memory Hill'), where there is a tall OBELISK [12]. On this prominent site on a hill high above the city, the first fortress on the Azores was built in 1474; nothing remains of it today. Its position far from the sea reflected a more traditional and Continental concept of mounting an acropolis defence, which was later given up in favour of modern fortresses closer to the sea. From up here, there is a magnificent view of Angra and its surroundings. The sheltered location of the harbour in the bay at the foot of Monte Brasil (*angra* meaning 'inlet' in Portuguese, hence the name of the city) is self-evident, as is the strategic position of the Fortaleza de São Filipe. From Angra's natural port, the city expanded inland along the slopes of a fertile valley. Even today green terraced fields cover the bottom of the valley; the municipal gardens are spread out in the lower basin. A stream used to flow through this valley, where nowadays the green pipes that feed a small hydroelectric power station can be seen. Its course was changed and channelled before 1474 to power the water mills of the flourishing industry — hence its name, Ribeira dos Moinhos.

Step back down into the municipal garden; its eastern side is dominated by the **Convento de São Francisco** [13]. This imposing monastic complex now houses the interesting Museum of Angra. Leave the garden above the Hotel Angra, climbing steeply along LADEIRA DE SÃO FRANCISCO past the entrance to the museum. Turn right into RUA DO CRUZEIRO at the road junction in front of a chapel. At the next junction, go down RUA DO GALO to the right, before forking sharply up left into RUA DA CONCEIÇÃO. If you look down Rua do Galo, which changes its name at the Praça Velha to Rua da Sé, you enjoy a beautiful view over the main street of Angra lined with attractive houses.

Just in front of you is a church in Renaissance style which was

Jardim Duque da Terceira, with the Convento de São Francisco in the background

built around 1533 on the site of a former hermitage, the **Igreja da Conceição** [14]. Turn right round the church and continue along RUA DO CONSELHEIRO MONJARDINO. Note the **Solar de N S dos Remédios** [15] on your right, a splendid manor house originally built in the 16th century (with later modifications) by the 'Armador' (Purveyor to the Royal Armadas). Located in **Corpo Santo** (the fishermen's district), it served as a warehouse for supplying provisions to ships from the West Indies and enabled quick access to the Porto das Pipas.

Continue ahead on RUA DO ARMADOR. Meet a T-junction where there is a good view of the harbour, the sheltered bay of Angra and Monte Brasil. Turn right downhill to meet another T-junction in front of the **Igreja da Misericórdia** [16], where you go left to the PATIO DA ALFÂNDEGA, the old customs quay. The church was built on the site of the Azores' first hospital, opened in 1492 thanks to the support of the Confraria do Santo Espírito (Brotherhood of the Holy Spirit). The present building, with its imposing baroque façade, dates from the 18th century and was built by the 'Misericórdia', a charity associated with a still-existing brotherhood. The hospital was relocated in the 19th century.

An imposing FLIGHT OF STEPS takes you down to the MARINA [17], which opened in 2000 to commemorate Angra's historical importance as a port town. Here in the sheltered Bay of Angra, vessels laden with gold and silver would lie at anchor from the **Porto das Pipas** (fishing harbour and quay for the ferries) and adjacent marina in the east to the small sandy cove in the west, on their long sea voyage from Spanish America to Lisbon, Cadiz or Seville. Where the flight of steps rises today, a fortified gate once permitted access to the city. The customs house or **Alfândega** [18] is still standing — once the city's most important building, since Angra owed most of its wealth to charging tolls.

From the Patio da Alfândega follow RUA DIREITA inland. Lined by traditional buildings with beautiful wrought-iron balconies, Angra's first main street will take you straight back from the quay to the Praça Velha. Built along Renaissance urban planning lines, this street forms an axis between the harbour and the central square of the city, thus opening it to the sea. Just before reaching the crossroads at the **Praça Velha**, note the beautiful stone-carved façade of the house on the left-hand corner, the **Casa do Conde Vilaflor** [19], now a pharmacy. It was built by the 11th Major General of the Azores and 7th Count of Vilaflor, a brave defender of liberal ideas. He led the liberal army into battle in 1829 at Praia and was also a member of the Regency established in Angra to defend the rights of progressive Queen Maria II against reactionary forces.

WALK 12 (TERCEIRA 2)

Serreta • Miradouro do Raminho • Cabo do Raminho • Ribeira do Veiga • Serreta

Distance/time: 9.8km/6.1mi; 3h15min
Grade: moderate. Good tracks with shady sections.
Equipment: see pages 47-48
How to get there and return: 🚌 Biscoitos bus from Angra; alight at the northern end of Serreta, just before reaching the edge of the woods, where the road to the lighthouse (yellow signpost 'Farol') turns off to the left. This is the second bus shelter past the village church and is on your right (the first

bus shelter past the church is on the left-hand side of the road). On your return, the bus departs some 35min later than from Biscoitos. By 🚗: coming from Angra, the turn-off to the lighthouse is a good 1km past the village church. There is a lay-by on the right-hand side of the road where you can leave your car.
Note: On your return to Angra you could take a bus via Praia da Vitória, making a stop in Biscoitos.
Photograph: Ponta do Raminho

For centuries the northwestern part of Terceira has been troubled by the volcanic eruptions typical of geologically unstable regions. In fact, new submarine activity has been recorded since December 1998 only 10km/6mi west of Serreta, where the magma has now risen to about 180 metres (600 feet) below sea level. Where the island has been partly inundated with lava in recent times, the rocky soil makes agriculture almost impossible, and so the woods have spread — an oasis of nature in the otherwise intensely-cultivated Terceiran landscape. This walk takes you high above the coast, through peaceful countryside, to the Ponta do Raminho, where there is an old whalers' look-out. You head back to Serreta along the wooded hillsides of the Serra de Santa Bárbara.

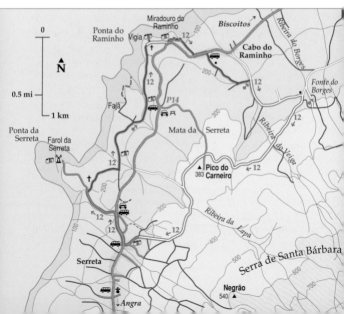

Start out at the BUS SHELTER at the end of **Serreta** by walking down the asphalt road signposted to the lighthouse ('FAROL'). When the road levels out, turn right on the gravel track and follow it through dense woodland, soon passing a SHRINE on the left. Turn left downhill when you meet a T-junction. Now you enjoy lovely views across pastures divided by stone walls. Down on the coast, the Ponta da Serreta and the lighthouse rising above it are seen; on a clear day, the islands of São Jorge and Graciosa are visible on the horizon. Pass a CATTLE TROUGH on the right and keep on the main track, undulating along the hillside. Soon you pass another CATTLE TROUGH on the right; bear right at the fork just beyond it (**30min**).

The track eventually rises across drier slopes. At the point where stones line the side of the track, look up to the right, to see a CROSS on a round stone base (easily missed). Almost immediately, the track bends to the right and levels out, leaving the steep coastline. After about 75m/yds take the path off left (by a rock), heading into the woods. You come upon an old WHALERS' LOOK-OUT POST almost immediately (*vigia*; see page 88).

Return to the main track and continue left to the coastal road at the **Miradouro do Raminho** (**1h**). Enjoy the beautiful view before heading on. Follow the road about 25m/yds to the left, then turn left through a gap in the wall, on a woodland path. This path descends steeply through the trees, occasionally on stone steps. Turn right uphill when it forks in front of the first pasture. After a few paces, bear left downhill, skirting a stone wall on your left almost immediately. Your path rises again, soon joining a field track which you follow to the right uphill between pastures.

Meet the coastal road again opposite the first house of **Cabo do Raminho** (**1h15min**) and turn left. At the THIRD HOUSE (No. 18), before reaching the bus shelter, turn right on the field track. Walk uphill between walled pastures and pass a cottage on the left; bear left at the fork shortly beyond it. Then pass orchards and walk through woods. After bearing left at another fork, you cross the bed of the **Ribeira do Veiga** (usually dried-out) and reach a FOUNTAIN ('CM 1946'; **1h35min**), with a cattle trough and WASH-HOUSE just beyond it. Here you turn right uphill at the T-junction.

Go up to the left at the next fork. Almost immediately, the track branches again; continue up to the left. When you reach a track junction in front of a terrace wall, continue straight ahead on the main track. Pastures blanket the surrounding slopes. On reaching a wide junction by a small stone building on the left, turn right uphill. Bear right again at the following fork. Now stay on the wide main track and follow it steadily uphill past any turn-offs. Soon leave the pastureland behind and continue through mixed woodland. Splendid fern trees thrive in the undergrowth and beside the track — growing wild.

Eventually you cross a small ASPHALT ROAD (**2h45min**) climbing from the picnic area Mata da Serreta and continue ahead on the track. About ten minutes later, go straight ahead past a wide turn on your right.

Emerging from the trees, you reach a wide track junction (**3h 05min**), where you turn right downhill. Keep following the main track steadily downhill; tar comes under foot by the first houses. On a clear day, you can see São Jorge on the horizon. The road you are on (CANADA DA FONTE) meets the main road opposite a BUS SHELTER in **Serreta** (**3h15min**). If you've come by car, turn right for five minutes to get back to the junction with the lighthouse road.

Walk 13 (Graciosa): landscape near Lagoa

WALK 13 (GRACIOSA 1)

Ribeirinha • Manuel Gaspar • Caldeirinha/Serra Branca • Canada Velha • Lagoa • Praia

See photograph opposite   **Distance/time**: 12.4km/7.7mi; 3h40min

Grade: easy. Gentle ascents and descents on country lanes and tracks. The short, but fairly steep ascent up the Caldeirinha crater is a detour that may be omitted.

Equipment: see pages 47-48; optional: bathing things

How to get there: 🚐 from Santa Cruz to Ribeirinha; alight at the church.
To return: 🚐 from Praia to Santa Cruz

Crossing Graciosa from the west coast to the east, you become acquainted with this idyllic island. Traditional whitewashed houses and old windmills are scattered over a gentle countryside crossed by a myriad of stone walls. You then wander through shady woodland and come upon strange walls, entrances and ruined houses in semi-darkness ... at some point they were abandoned; now nature has recaptured and almost completely overgrown the once-cultivated area. Your destination is the village of Praia with its small sandy beach.

The walk starts at the CHURCH in **Ribeirinha**, where there is a bandstand in the middle of the roundabout. Follow the street at the left of the church (signposted to ALTO RIBEIRINHA and BRASILEIRA). It runs uphill past houses and skirts the volcano Caldeiras; there is a beautiful view towards Vitória in the north. Meet a T-junction, where you continue to the right. A fertile plain divided by numerous stone walls extends to the left; it is mainly used as grazing land for cattle. At the highest point in the road, a ruined WINDMILL with two old millstones is seen on the right (**30min**).

Soon meet another T-junction where you turn left. Follow this road for barely 200m/yds, until it forks, then bear right for 'MANUEL GASPAR' and ignore a track off to the left after some 70m/yds. You climb through the strung-out village of **Manuel Gaspar**. Soon after the last houses are behind you, the road sweeps to the left; some buildings are on the right. Here take the tarred lane that climbs up right towards the wind generators on the hill. But before you follow this lane uphill, you should have a look at the buildings on your right. Below a cistern and an open water tank (the 'TANQUE VELHO' of Almas), there is an old wash-house with washstands and two old ox carts (**1h20min**).

Now follow the tarred lane uphill, soon bearing right at a fork. The lane climbs steeply to a SADDLE on top of the **Serra Branca** (**1h45min**). Wind-driven electricity generators (the 'PARQUE EÓLICO GRACIOSA') stand on the hill to the left, while there's a small rise on your right with a TRIG POINT inscribed 'IGC 1938'. Go towards it and follow the gravel track round the crater rim; the steep crater basin, **Caldeirinha**, opens up quite unexpectedly. Enjoy the magnificent panorama from the crater rim — the neighbouring islands of São Jorge, Pico and Faial can be seen.

When you've rounded the crater, facing the entrance to the

Parque Eólico, follow the minor track that begins on your right. It begins to lead downhill, soon narrowing to a cows' path. Continue to descend in the direction of a pond seen ahead in the distance and pass an old WATER TANK on your right; then the path gets wider again as it leads back to the TANQUE VELHO.

Return to the wide sweep of the asphalt road and follow it past the POND which is seen on the left, slightly below the road. Leave the road before reaching the first houses of Almas and turn right on a wide field track. This main track (called CANADA VELHA) runs almost straight through walled pastureland. The long ridge of the Serra das Fontes rises beyond the valley on your left, while the slopes to the right belong to the Serra Dormida (the 'Sleeping Ridge'), culminating in Pico Timão, at 398m/1305ft the highest peak on the island.

About half an hour after leaving the Tanque Velho the track gains an asphalt surface. Leave it almost immediately where it bends to the left and continue ahead on the GRAVEL TRACK (**2h30min**).

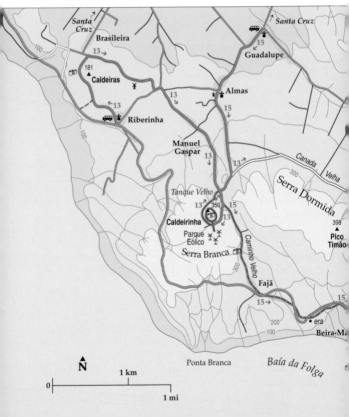

Very soon you pass a small QUARRY on the left and a minor track joining from the right. Your track begins to descend through woodland. When the trees thin out and the track bends sharp left, rising slightly, take a minor grassy track down to the right. Soon join an ASPHALT ROAD (**2h45min**).

Turn right for some 50m/yds, until a track turns off sharp left. Now stay ahead on this main track, which runs through woodland past old drystone walls and entrances. Most of the gardens and fields hiding behind these walls are abandoned. Nature has reclaimed this once-cultivated area, which is now almost completely overgrown. Quite unexpectedly, you come upon a massive, but abandoned MANOR HOUSE (dating from 1940) with high protective walls (*quinta;* **3h**). At the track junction here, continue in the same direction, skirting the manor house. When you meet a T-junction, turn right downhill. The old trail you are on is running along the lower slopes of the **Serra das Fontes**. Its name is CANADA DO NEVOEIRO, which means 'trail of dense fog'. Sections of the trail

Crossed by a plethora of stone walls, a gentle countryside unfolds, with cows grazing on the pastures.

are stone-cobbled, and grooves from the wheels of the heavy ox carts used for centuries to carry crops down to the villages are still evident (an ox cart can be seen in the Santa Cruz museum).

Meet an asphalt road and follow it to the right for some 20m/yds, then turn left on a track that is tarred at the outset. This field track runs in the middle of a sheltered valley, with orchards and fields on either side. You pass the CHURCH of Sant' Ana in **Lagoa** (**3h20min**). Go straight on past a right turn. Reach a T-junction a few minutes later and turn right. Follow this road, which is lined by houses, to the wide road junction at the entrance to **Praia** (**3h35min**) and continue straight ahead. Note the QUINTA DAS ALMAS on the left, a beautiful old manor house. A few minutes later, the road enters the village by a CHURCH (1812); there is a BUS SHELTER on your left (**3h40min**). If you have time, head straight to the beach, or turn right along RUA RODRIGUES SAMPAIO (past another old church) to visit the MAIN CHURCH.

Whaling boats in the harbour at Lajes on Pico. The same type of boat has been used for centuries.

WHALE-WATCHING POSTS

During the whaling era, when the Azorean whalers were hunting sperm whales *(baleias)*, a very effective signal system was in use. Commanding a good view over the sea, look-out posts *(vigias de baleia;* see photograph page 20) were built above the coastlines around the islands. The window of these bunker-like cabins is just a slit — otherwise the look-out *(vigia)* would be blinded by the glare of the sun on the water, as he searched the horizon for the give-away signs of the whales — their water spouts. When he saw any whales, the *vigia* made smoke signals or fired rockets. The whalers immediately abandoned any other work and ran down to the nearest harbour. While these courageous men set out to the sea in tiny boats, the signal man *(sinalizador)* started work. He ran up flags on the roof of the look-out post or unfurled big pieces of cloth, to show the whalers which way to go. Only in more recent times has radio contact replaced this old method of signalling.

In accordance with the international agreement on species protection, whaling was discontinued in the Azores in the 1980s.

There are whaling museums in Lajes do Pico and Santa Cruz da Graciosa.

WALK 14 (GRACIOSA 2)

Canada Longa • Furna do Abel • Furna Maria Encantada • Caldeira • Furna do Enxofre • Luz

See map pages 86-87

Distance/time: 12.1km/7.5mi; 3h55min

Grade: easy. The walk leads along little-used country lanes, with an overall ascent of 330m/1080ft.

Equipment: see pages 47-48. A torch is also useful (although not essential) when walking through the road tunnel into the crater: it's 140m/yds long, and there is no electric lighting.

How to get there: 🚌 Luz bus from Santa Cruz; get off the bus at the bus stop 'Canada Longa' (there is a metal bus shelter here)

To return: 🚌 from Luz to Santa Cruz

Shorter walk: Caldeira circuit and Furna do Enxofre from Canada Longa (11km/6.8mi; 3h30min). Grade, equipment, access as above. Or by 🚗: park near the bus shelter at Canada Longa. Follow the main walk to the Furna do Enxofre (2h50min), then return straight ahead on the Caldeira road back to Canada Longa.

Opening hours

Furna do Enxofre: open daily *(1 June to 30 September only)* from 11.00-15.00; there is a small entrance fee. Out of season, arrange for a visit 24 hours in advance at the Câmara Municipal in Santa Cruz.

LAVA TUNNELS

Lava tunnels *(furnas)* were formed after a volcanic eruption when the pressure eased and the molten lava began to flow more slowly. The surface of the lava stream began to cool down and harden, while the inside remained liquid. When this lava stopped flowing, an empty tunnel was left behind.

On the inner walls, traces of the flowing lava, including edges and ledges, are seen where the lava flow made a bend. Quite often short 'stalactites' of dripping lava which has solidified hang down from the ceiling.

These tunnels can run for kilometres through the mountainsides. Sometimes short sections have fallen in (as at the Furna Maria Encantada shown above), giving access to these hall-like subterranean galleries.

Photograph: the Furna Maria Encantada. Some parts of this lava tunnel have collapsed, so sunlight falls into it.

This exciting walk takes you around the outer slopes of Graciosa's *caldeira*. You enjoy wonderful views out over the island itself and, if visibility is good, you will see all the other islands of the central group ... one after another. Then you descend to the bottom of the secluded crater basin, framed by steep wooded slopes. Inside the crater lies the famous Furna do Enxofre, a huge cave 220m long and 120m wide (720 by 395 feet), with a subterranean fresh-water lake at its bottom. Prince Albert of Monaco, who conducted marine research in the 19th century, was one of the first visitors to abseil into the cave in 1879. He described the cavern as 'one of the wonders of the world'. In 1939, the present spiral staircase with its 184 steps was built, giving tourists easier access to the cave.

Start out at the BUS STOP **Canada Longa**. Walk back on the main street towards Praia for some 50m/yds; then turn right on the road signposted 'CALDEIRA'. Soon you leave the last houses behind and walk gently uphill amidst

89

View to Luz from the Caldeira circuit

walled pastures. Bear right at a fork. After the FIFTH ELECTRICITY MAST, where the road bends left, ignore a field track off right (your return route). Just past it, you come upon an interesting volcanic phenomenon on the right: the **Furna do Abel** (**20min**; see page 89).

Continuing uphill, you pass a PIGGERY on the right and a WATER TANK on the left. Soon reach a road junction where you turn left. After some 100m/yds, climb steps on your right up to the **Furna Maria Encantada** ('Enchanted Maria's Cavern'), yet another spectacular lava tunnel running right through the rim of the crater (**40min**). If you turn right through the tunnel, you reach a vantage point with a fine view out over the huge crater basin but, from up here, nothing reveals its amazing treasure, the great subterranean sulphur cavern.

Return down the steps to the gravel road and continue to the right, circling clockwise round the **Caldeira**. Some benches invite you to rest while enjoying the magnificent view. Initially, you look down onto Praia and the islet off the coast; then there is a sweeping view past the lighthouse (Farol da Restinga) and the Ilhéu de Baixo to the neighbouring island of Terceira, rising on the horizon if it's a clear day. Later you can see Carapacho down on the coast and the island of São Jorge in the south. Eventually, the steep coastline at Baía da Folga, with its pale cliffs comes into sight, as well as the wind generators on the Serra Branca.

Reach the ROAD JUNCTION again where your circuit began (**2h 05min**). Bear left and follow the road downhill past the Furna do Abel. After some ten minutes, turn right on the road that runs from the Canada Longa to the Caldeira and follow it gently uphill. Go through the SHORT TUNNEL (**2h30min**) and ignore the left turn just beyond the exit (it leads to Picnic 16). Follow the road down to the crater basin and the **Furna do Enxofre** ('Sulphur Cavern'; **2h50min**). The vapours from some bubbling springs have given the cave its name. The lake is up to 14m/50ft deep.

After exploring the famous sulphur cavern, return the same way to the field track that turns off right just before the Furna do Abel (the 20min-point on the outward leg; **3h35min**). *(But for the Shorter walk, return straight ahead from the cavern on the Caldeira road, back to Canada Longa.)* Follow this track; there is another view to the left down into the cave. At the first house, the field track turns into a small road. Meet the main road and turn left downhill into **Luz** (**3h55min**). The BUS STOP and a restaurant are by the main road junction in the village centre; a little further on, to the left, is the CHURCH.

WALK 15 (GRACIOSA 3)

Guadalupe • Almas • Beira-Mar • Luz

See map pages 86-87   **Distance/time:** 8.9km/5.5mi; 3h

Grade: easy walk along field tracks and little-used asphalt lanes, with an overall ascent of 310m/1020ft.

Equipment: see pages 47-48; optional: bathing things

How to get there: 🚌 from Santa Cruz to Guadalupe; get off at the village church
To return: 🚌 from the main crossroads in Luz back to Santa Cruz

This walk follows an old cobbled trail along the slopes of the Serra Branca and down to Baía da Folga. En route you pass old stone houses and solitary farms standing between terraced fields and pastures. Down on the rocky coastline you come upon the hamlet of Beira-Mar with its black-lava houses. Only a few years ago it had been abandoned almost completely and the buildings were left to fall into ruin, but now the houses are being restored one after another. There is a magnificent vista from here, towards the steep coastline with its sheer cliffs that rise up to 300m/1000ft.

Start out at the MAIN ROAD JUNCTION in **Guadalupe**. Follow the road past the imposing CHURCH, heading towards 'ALMAS/RIBEI-RINHA'. The church was severely damaged by an earthquake in 1989; it took four years to rebuild it. Soon, ignore a right turn and climb ahead through **Almas**. The village street is lined by new and old houses, some of which have beautiful gardens. Steadily rising, ignore another right turn. Almost immediately, you pass a small church on the left and a CHAPEL dedicated to the Holy Ghost on the right (an *império;* see page 39).

Beyond the last, rather shabby houses, you pass a gravel road forking off sharp left and a POND on the right. Soon the road forks opposite some buildings. Below a cistern and an open WATER TANK (the TANQUE VELHO; **1h**), there is an old wash-house with wash-stands and two old ox carts. Turn left uphill at the fork; some wind generators producing electricity stand on the hill ahead. Reach another fork after some 200m/yds, where you keep left (Walk 13 bears right here), following a field track between walled pastures. The slopes to the left belong to the Serra Branca, while the Serra Dormida (the 'Sleeping Ridge') rises to the right, culminating in Pico Timão, at 398m/1305ft the highest peak on the island.

Ignore a left turn and continue ahead. The field track soon narrows into an old cobbled trail (CAMINHO VELHO) and begins to descend steadily. On a clear day, you can see the neighbouring island of São Jorge stretching out on the horizon. Further downhill, you pass a small group of partly-derelict stone houses called **Fajã** (**1h30min**). Some buildings have been carefully renovated and are now used as summer holiday homes. Meet a road, cross it and continue down the old trail just opposite. There is another big house on the left that has been renovated by emigrants.

Cross the road again, this time diagonally to the right, and go up the tarred side-road. Leave it almost immediately where it bends left and continue ahead on the trail, soon passing a farm. Cross the road once more and find the continuation of the trail just opposite. Note the old circular THRESHING FLOOR (*era*) on your right. (If rubbish has been dumped on the trail, you can avoid this section by climbing the earthen bank up to the road.) The trail joins the road again; now follow it down to the right.

Soon take a sharp right turn and descend a gravel track (possibly asphalted in the near future) lined by lamp-posts. It ends at a turning area in front of an electricity sub-station by some renovated houses in **Beira-Mar** ('Seashore'; **2h**). An old trail continues to the right, sections of which are roughly cobbled. It winds down along crumbling drystone walls built of black lava to the rocky coastline. Grooves from the wheels of heavy ox carts used for centuries to carry crops to the village are still evident. The crop was probably not abundant, judging from the small stony enclosures between the dark lava walls, most of them now overgrown. Only vines seem to thrive in this parched and sun-baked terrain.

The old trail peters out on the rocky coast. You can bathe in the rock pools here or find your own private picnic spot in the overgrown lava fields extending inland. There is a sweeping view over Baía da Folga to the pale cliffs at Ponta Branca, rising almost sheer over 300m/1000ft. When a strong southwesterly blows, the Atlantic pounds this steep coastline relentlessly.

Return the same way to the main road and follow it to the right. Soon you reach the first houses of **Limeira** and meet a T-junction, where you turn right. Continue ahead past the right turn to the Farol da Folga, to reach the main road junction (with BUS STOP) in **Luz** (**3h**). The 'Golden King' serves meals and snacks. It's also worth visiting the CHURCH: go down the road from the junction and turn left almost immediately. There's a sunny terrace in front of the church, with a magnificent view across the sea to São Jorge.

Beira-Mar

WALK 16 (SÃO JORGE 1)

Parque Sete Fontes • Farol de Rosais • Ponta de Rosais • Parque Sete Fontes

See also photograph page 22
Distance/time: 12.2km/7.6mi; 3h 40min
Grade: easy; mostly level walking along good tracks; overall ascent of 310m/1020ft
Equipment: see pages 47-48
How to get there and return: 🚗 taxi or car from Velas to/from the chapel in the Parque Sete Fontes picnic area (9.5km). Leave Velas on the main road and take the signposted left turn to Rosais. Go straight ahead past the village church in Rosais for another 300m, before heading right uphill at the fork. Turn left at the junction in the highlands; this road leads direct to the picnic area. Or 🚌 from Velas to/from Ponta de Rosais (journey time 25min). The bus first passes the village church (*igreja*) in Rosais, before reaching the road junction at the old milk-collection point in Ponta de Rosais five

minutes later. Get off the bus here and begin the walk at the 2h45min-point. *Note:* the bus continues several hundred metres past this point, to where the road turns sharply right and the track from the lighthouse comes in from the left.

Short walk: Parque Sete Fontes — Ponta de Rosais — Parque Sete Fontes (4km 2.5mi; 1h30min). Grade, equipment and access as above. Follow the main walk initially, but keep left at the 10min-point. After 200m/yds you reach a wide track junction where you turn left. This track runs straight down to Ponta de Rosais. From the milk-collection point (the 2h45min-point in the main walk), follow the notes back to the Parque Sete Fontes.

Photograph: the reddish gravel track on the plateau, lined with hydrangeas and heather trees

A fascinating feeling of solitude and space envelops you as you walk through green pastureland across the rolling highlands of São Jorge to the lighthouse at Ponta de Rosais, the most westerly tip of the island. Wonderful views over the sea and the neighbouring islands of Graciosa, Pico and Faial accompany you all the way. Only the coast of São Jorge itself remains hidden, because of the sheer drop from the highlands down to the shore.

The enchanting **Parque Sete Fontes** ('Seven Springs'; Picnic 18), is a picnic area on the western highlands, lovingly laid out in wooded surroundings reminiscent of a fairy-tale forest. There is a wide road junction here, with a CHAPEL and a STONE MODEL of the island with a boat, donated by emigrants. **Start out*** by following the REDDISH GRAVEL TRACK that continues between the chapel on the right and the shelter on the left. Soon you pass a plaque on the embankment to the left; continue ahead, ignoring the left turn just beyond it. Reach a fork in the track where you bear right (**10min**). *(The Short walk continues to the left here.)* Soon go straight ahead

---

*Before heading off, you could first make a side-trip to a viewpoint: follow the tarmac track to the right of the chapel and bear left at a fork after 100m/yds. In some 5min this gravel track leads to a turning place, from where a footpath descends to a small viewpoint with a brilliant view of the north coast.

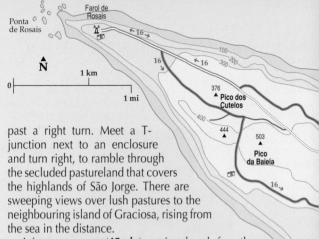

Ponta
de Rosais

Farol de
Rosais

←16

16

←16

100
200
300

▲N

1 km

0

1 mi

376
▲ Pico dos
Cutelos

400

444
▲

503
▲
Pico
da Baieia

16→

past a right turn. Meet a T-junction next to an enclosure and turn right, to ramble through the secluded pastureland that covers the highlands of São Jorge. There are sweeping views over lush pastures to the neighbouring island of Graciosa, rising from the sea in the distance.

Join a WIDER TRACK (**45min**) coming sharply from the left and continue to the right. This track runs arrow-straight towards the lighthouse, soon crossing a wooded area mainly covered with heather trees. When the woodland ends on your left and pastures begin, a track turns off sharp left by a CATTLE TROUGH; you will be taking it on your way back. But for now carry straight on until you reach the **Farol de Rosais** (**1h**). Its buildings were damaged during the 1980 earthquake and then abandoned — it's an eerie sight. There is a path to the left of the turning circle just in front of the buildings which leads to a breathtaking viewpoint towards Ponta de Rosais, the most westerly point on São Jorge. Sheer cliffs fall down to the sea; off the coast there are some rocky islets. The neighbouring islands of Pico and Faial can be seen to the southwest.

Return the same way until you reach the edge of the woodland, where you bear right on the side track, beginning a gradual but steady ascent. Ignore a minor track turning off sharp right. Very soon, turn right at WIDE JUNCTION (**2h**; just before the highest point in the track). Crossing the ridge, you begin to descend on the southern side of São Jorge. A stunning panorama unravels, with Pico and Faial rising from the sea.

The track undulates along the hillside and leads through a wooded area. Ahead of you, the São Jorge's central mountain ridge, with its numerous volcanic cones, extends to the east. Continue ahead when you reach the asphalted village street in **Ponta de Rosais**. Note the old communal WASHING PLACE on the left and the old FOUNTAIN (built in 1887) just past it. Ignore the left turn at the old milk-collection point (LACTICÍNIOS DE SÃO JORGE LDA/POSTO DE DESNATAÇÃO; **2h45min**) and continue ahead on the village street. (*If you get to the walk by bus, start out and end the walk here; the Short walk joins from the left at this point.*)

Note another big FOUNTAIN (this one was built in 1874) with cattle-trough and WASH-HOUSE on the left-hand side of the road (**2h55min**). Soon, turn sharp left on a track that is concreted at the outset; it rises past some houses on the slopes of **Pico da Velha**. As you ascend, you enjoy a beautiful view of Rosais. Pass a right turn and continue to climb. Soon the route swings right and you're immersed in the low woodlands that cover the upper slopes of Pico da Velha. Eventually you join a track and carry straight on until you meet an asphalt road. Turn left, back to the CHAPEL at the **Parque Sete Fontes** (3h40min).

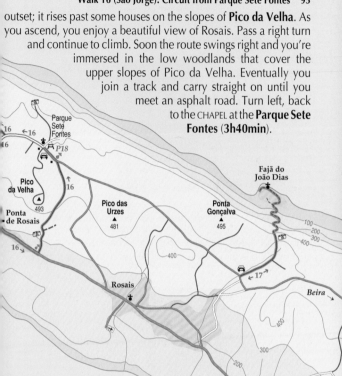

CORY'S SHEARWATER

Very common throughout the seas of the Azores, Cory's Shearwater (*Calonectris diomedea ssp borealis*; Portuguese *cagarro*) superficially resembles a gull, but is a relative of the albatross. There are about 20 different species of Shearwater, large petrels of the genera *Calonectris* and *Puffinus*, all of which have the habit of skimming just above the surface of the ocean — hence their name. Cory's Shearwater is a grey-brown species that breeds on islands in the eastern

Atlantic and the Mediterranean. After breeding, the birds migrate in autumn to winter on the American coast and in the Southern Atlantic, returning in March.

Cory's Shearwater is superbly adapted to an offshore life, always feeding, resting and mating at sea, where it also floats on the surface of the water. On land it is awkward and vulnerable, and it only comes ashore to nest. Cory's Shearwater breeds in colonies and digs its nesting tunnel in cliffs and rocky offshore islets, visiting the nest only

during the night. During daylight, one may not notice the birds, even when present in large colonies. The female lays a single egg in May which is bred by both parents for 55 days. Breeding birds which have been out searching for food return home at dusk and as soon as it gets dark fly around with strange hoarse and husky cries which can be heard all night.

The bird becomes sexually mature at the age of seven, and younger birds that do not breed, may spend years at sea without landing at all.

WALK 17 (SÃO JORGE 2)

Fajã do João Dias

See map pages 94-95
Distance/time: 6km/3.7mi; 2h45min
Grade: moderate. Steep, but not vertiginous cliff path, with a descent and corresponding ascent of 400m/1310ft.
Equipment: see pages 47-48; optional: bathing things
How to get there and return: only accessible by 🚕 taxi or car; 11km from Velas. Leave Velas on the main road and take the signposted left turn to Rosais. Go straight ahead past the village church in Rosais for another 300m, then turn right uphill at the fork in the road. Turn right at the junction in the highlands (signposted 'Fajã do João Dias'). After 2.5km a gravel track turns off left (by a glazed tile inscribed 'Fajã do João Dias'); this turn-off comes up about 50m before a wide gravel road turns off right. Leave your car by the roadside, well tucked in. (Note: You could also drive to this walk via Beira: 1.5 km past the main crossroads in the village, turn left at a chapel. Then keep right until the signposted gravel track turns off right.)

Photograph: Fajã do João Dias

The north coast of São Jorge drops abruptly and dramatically over 400m/1300ft into the sea, with dense vegetation clinging to the cliffs. Inaccessible by car, Fajã do João Dias lies down by the sea, isolated from the outside world. A mere handful of houses stands on the small coastal strip, but some are still inhabited year-round. The hamlet's only connection with the rest of the island is via an old footpath that was skillfully built, winding up the cliffs. You can still see heavily-burdened mules on the path. If the sea is calm, a small fishing boat can come to drop anchor in the bay and its beautiful sandy cove.

Start out on the gravel track by the glazed tile, 'FAJÃ DO JOÃO DIAS'. At first the rolling pastureland around you hides the dramatic cliffs from view. Hedgerows of heather trees and hydrangeas line the fields that cover the slopes on your right. Follow the main track until it ends at a small car park. Go through the GREEN IRON GATE (**15min**) and join the old footpath, sections of which are still cobbled. It winds its way down the cliffs through dense vegetation. There is a magnificent view of the steep coastline, with the *fajã* some 400/1300ft below you.

The footpath descends through dense greenery. Continue straight ahead past a sharp left turn. When you reach a fork you have the choice: you can either go straight ahead or turn sharp right; the paths rejoin. Eventually, the trees begin to thin out and you look straight down onto the *fajã* (coastal plain; see page 104) below.

The path descends past terraced vineyards and houses to the coast. Once down in **Fajã do João Dias**, follow the coastal path to the CHAPEL and on between houses to the sandy BEACH (**1h15min**).

After a refreshing swim in the ocean, retrace your steps to the gravel track by the glazed tile, 'FAJÃ DO JOÃO DIAS' (**2h45min**).

WALK 18 (SÃO JORGE 3)

Velas • Portal do Cedro • Pico das Caldeirinhas • Santo António

See also photograph page 24   **Distance/time**: 15.4km/9.6mi; 5h30min

Grade: moderate, with a long ascent of 800m/2625ft and a gentle descent. *But note*: because of the altitude, this walk should only be tackled on cloudless days or when there are only high clouds.

Equipment: see pages 47-48

How to get there: the walk begins in the municipal park at Velas, at the bandstand shown on page 99.

To return: 🚌 from Santo António's church back to Velas

Shorter walk: Velas — Pico das Caldeirinhas (11.6km/7.2mi; 4h30min). Grade and access as above; return by 🚕 pre-arranged taxi from Pico das Caldeirinhas (the highest point on the Urzelina/Santo António road). Follow the main walk until you meet the road at Pico das Caldeirinhas. Omit the descent to Santo António. If you prefer to descend, this walk can be done in reverse with careful reference to the map, but make sure you chose a fine day with good visibility.

This walk leads across the hilly high-mountain region of São Jorge — an extremely isolated landscape, often shrouded in mist due to its high altitude. The meadows up here are particularly lush and green, and amidst luxuriant hydrangea hedges there are marvellous specimens of the Azorean heather tree *(Erica azorica)* to be seen. En route you enjoy marvellous views of all the neighbouring islands of the central group.

Start out at the small MUNICIPAL GARDEN with bandstand in **Velas**. From its northern corner, follow RUA DE SANTO ANDRÉ uphill. Turn

Landscape at the Portal do Cedro, with blue-flowering hydrangea hedgerows

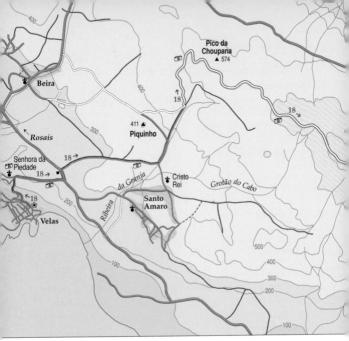

right into RUA DO ROQUE AFONSO just past the courthouse on your right (inscribed 'DOMUS IUSTITIAE'). At the end of this street, you climb steeply on a stepped footpath past hillside houses. Meet a concrete road and follow it uphill to the right. Leave it just past a beautiful old house with a fountain and bear left uphill on the old cobbled trail. Then you join an asphalt road opposite the church of Senhora da Piedade; turn right uphill. As you ascend the road, there are fine views of Velas and over the strait to Pico.

Meet a T-JUNCTION (**50min**) and turn left on the main road, but leave it very soon by turning right on the gravel track opposite the driveway to a house. After a short while, ignore a left turn and continue ahead. Again, stay ahead on the main track when you reach the next fork. There is a beautiful view on your right over pastures to the village of Santo Amaro. Meet a T-JUNCTION (**1h30min**) and turn left uphill on the road; soon Japanese red cedars (*Cryptomeria japonica*) line the roadside. Then turn right on the gravel track that ascends along the edge of the cedar wood.

When you reach a WIDE JUNCTION (**2h**), continue uphill on the asphalt road. When the asphalt runs out after 10 minutes, continue on the gravel track. You will be following this main track for the next hour and half as it runs steadily uphill along São Jorge's central mountain ridge. There are magnificent views out over green pastureland criss-crossed by hedgerows with blue hydrangeas and splendid specimens of tree heather. Cows graze peacefully in the meadows. Across the strait, the neighbouring islands of Faial and Pico rise from an indigo sea, dominated by the majestic volcano.

On reaching a wide fork in the track at the **Portal do Cedro**

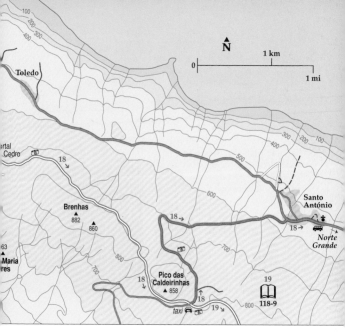

(**3h30min**), just past a building on your right, keep straight ahead. Soon you cross the central ridge of peaks, to continue the climb on the northern side of the island. There are pleasant views out over green pastures criss-crossed by a myriad of hydrangea hedges down to Toledo (an old hamlet founded by the Spanish); far out to sea you can make out the neighbouring islands of Graciosa and Terceira on a clear day. Above you, the slopes rise to the summit of Brenhas ('Wilderness').

The track begins to descend and skirts the **Pico das Caldeirinhas** before meeting an ASPHALT ROAD (**4h30min**). *(The Shorter walk ends here; Walk 19 begins on the gravel track opposite.)* There is an interesting view to the right into several volcanic craters that erupted only a few centuries ago; the black cinder is covered by low tree heather. Turn left on the asphalt road and ignore a track to the right a few minutes later. Lined by hydrangea hedges, the road descends steadily; Graciosa and Terceira are seen ahead. Bear right at the junction with the main road, to walk on into the centre of **Santo António**, a typical Azorean village set amongst fields and flowers. The BUS SHELTER is just in front of the CHURCH (**5h30min**).

Bandstand (coreto) at Velas

WALK 19 (SÃO JORGE 4)

Pico das Caldeirinhas • Pico da Esperança • Norte Grande • Fajã do Ouvidor

Distance/time: 20km/12.4mi; 4h45min

Grade: moderate, with a gradual ascent of 250m/820ft on a gravel track to Pico da Esperança and a long descent of 1050m/3445ft on track and road. *But note:* because of the altitude, this walk should only be tackled on cloudless days or when there are only high clouds.

Equipment: see pages 47-48; optional: bathing things

How to get there: by ⊟ (taxi) to Pico das Caldeirinhas (the highest point on the Urzelina/Santo António road). Most taxi drivers know the spot.

To return: by ⊟ (pre-arranged taxi) from Fajã do Ouvidor; a good meeting point is the car park/bar above the harbour.

Pico da Esperança

This walk leads along the central ridge of the island to Pico da Esperança, the highest summit on São Jorge. This high mountain region is often shrouded in mist, so pick a cloudless day to enjoy the splendid views, reaching out to all neighbouring islands of the central group. You will pass through the village of Norte Grande before descending to Fajã do Ouvidor, a magnificent coastal plain with a small harbour. The name of this *fajã* dates back to the times of the monarchy, when an *ouvidor*, or 'listener', settled here. Each of the islands had such an official with his 'ear to the ground', who informed the king of local problems before things got out of hand.

Start out opposite **Pico das Caldeirinhas** on the URZELINA/SANTO ANTÓNIO ROAD: turn right (east) up the gravel track. Pico do Pedro (901m/2955ft) rises to your right. Pass a DUCK POND on the right (**45min**). About half an hour later, there is a plaque on the left commemorating the victims of a plane crash in 1999. Then you pass a small CRATER LAKE on your right (**1h30min**) and cross a small dam. Soon you pass a plaque inscribed 'PICO DA ESPERANÇA' on the left. Take a sharp left turn just 100m/yds past the plaque and follow this minor track uphill. Soon after a right-hand bend, you will see another crater lake on your left. The track now peters out; continue to climb in an anti-clockwise direction on the grassy rim of the crater, until you reach the TRIG POINT ('IGC 1937') on the highest point of **Pico da Esperança** ('Peak of Hope' 1053m/3454ft; **2h**).

Return to the main track and turn left to continue. The next distinct volcano is **Pico do Arieiro** (**2h50min**). A short time later, an abandoned QUARRY with lichen-covered rocks appears on the right. Almost immediately, **Pico Pinheiro** rises on the right; to the left you can see a partially-collapsed lava tunnel (see page 89). Turn

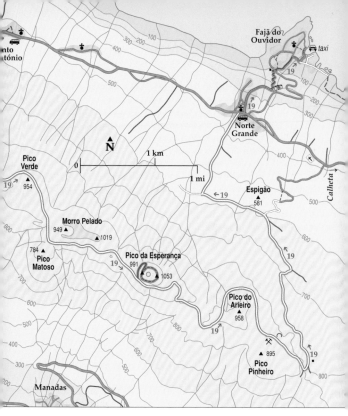

left at a FORK (**3h05min**) and pass a sharp right turn almost at once. Soon you cross a CATTLE GRID; a building used by the shepherds is on the right. Cross another CATTLE GRID after some 400m/yds.

Bear left when you reach ANOTHER FORK (**3h25min**). Turn left again at the next T-junction. When you reach another junction after 100m/yds, bear left (almost straight) uphill. This track contours along the hillside, undulating slightly. Take the first major turn on your right (**3h45min**); this forks sharply to the right and runs straight downhill. Ignore a minor right turn and follow the main track down to **Norte Grande**, where you meet the main road just opposite the village church, by a BUS SHELTER (**4h05min**).

Turn right for a few paces, then go left down the street just in front of the church. Keep straight ahead to a VIEWPOINT (**4h15min**) from where you enjoy a splendid view down onto Fajã do Ouvidor. Descend the cobbled path on the left, winding steeply downhill through lush vegetation. The path widens to a track by a WATER-PUMPING BUILDING and tank. Soon cross a road diagonally to the right and continue to descend on the gravel track. You reach a crossroads with a plane tree in the middle just past the first houses of **Fajã do Ouvidor** (**4h35min**). Turn right at the crossroads and follow the road (with fine views down to the coast), then continue on the cliff path to the HARBOUR (**4h45min**).

WALK 20 (SÃO JORGE 5)

Serra do Topo • Caldeira de Cima • Fajã da Caldeira de Santo Cristo • Fajã dos Tijolos • Fajã do Belo • Fajã dos Cubres

See also photographs pages 17, 105   **Distance/time:** 8.7km/5.4mi; 3h40min

Grade: moderate. First there is a steady descent from an altitude of 700m/2300ft down to sea level, then the walk undulates along the coastline. Note that on the high-mountain region (Serra do Topo) where the walk begins, you have to reckon with low clouds and mist, but it usually clears up when you descend. The route is waymarked with yellow and red flashes.

Equipment: see pages 47-48; optional: bathing things

How to get there: 🚕 taxi from Velas (34.5km). Taxi drivers usually know where to drop you when you tell them that you want to walk from the Serra do Topo down to the Fajã da Caldeira (de Santo Cristo). If friends are taking you to the starting point, the driver should follow the main road from Velas towards Topo. Some 5.5km beyond the right-hand turning to Ribeira Seca, a wide gravel road from Norte Pequeno joins the main road from the left. The main road then bends to the right and, after some 200m/yds there is a concrete bus shelter ('SRHE 1997') on the right. Opposite it, a field track turns off to the left, signposted to the various *fajãs*. (Access by bus is not practicable; bus times are inconvenient.) *To return:* 🚕 taxi back to Velas (29km). Arrange in advance to be picked up at the bar opposite the church in Fajã dos Cubres.

Note: The number of wooden gates may change in the future.

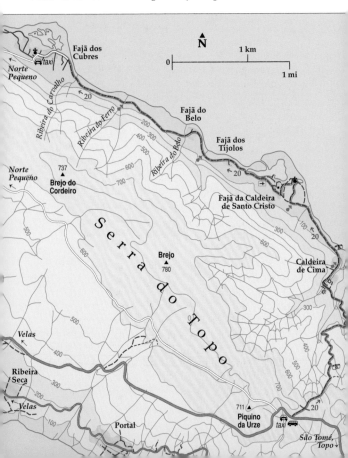

It takes some effort to get there, but this walk is one of the best in all the Azores — don't miss it! The landscapes are simply fantastic, with breathtaking views all the way. From the pastureland of the high-mountain region you descend to the steep north coast on small paths and old cobbled trails, via the wild and romantic valley of the Caldeira de Cima. Then you wander at the foot of steep cliffs from *fajã* to *fajã* — small coastal plains with traditional hamlets and fertile orchards. By the way: *caldeira* means 'cauldron' in Portuguese. On the Azores the term usually refers to a volcanic crater but, in this case, it is used to refer to the ravine-like valley, mainly created by erosion.

Begin the walk on the hilly high-mountain region of São Jorge that is often enveloped in clouds; here it is called **Serra do Topo** (see photograph page 105). Pass the official TOURIST INFORMATION BOARD and go through the gate, to follow the field track up to the top of the ridge, where there is a cow-milking place. From up here, you overlook the mighty ravine-like valley of the Caldeira de Cima (unless it's misty!), its slopes covered with lush pastures ribboned with hydrangea hedges. Dense woods cloak the steeper flanks.

Now follow the old trail, descending slightly to the right between hydrangeas; it's partly cobbled or stepped and well waymarked with red and yellow flashes. Soon you come upon a shelter carved into the rock to your right. Walk through a WOODEN GATE and pass another shelter on your right. The trail snakes steadily downhill, and you go through another GATE. Eventually walk through one more GATE and descend a few stone steps just beyond it. Splendid specimens of tree heather flourish on the hillside; the island of Graciosa is seen ahead on the distant horizon.

Walk through yet another wooden GATE. The path now descends towards the river bed, and you can hear the sound of running water. Just before reaching the river bed, your path bends sharp right; ignore the wooden gate on the left. Down in the valley you can make out terraced fields and some ruined houses — your next destination. The path continues to descend between pastures along the hillside to the right. Go through a GATE in a wooded side-valley and cross a STREAM; another STREAM is crossed almost immediately. Now continue downhill through dense vegetation on the old trail; it soon gains a cobbled surface.

Eventually you reach the BRIDGE (**1h30min**) leading across the main river — the ideal place for taking a breather. There are rock pools in the river — most inviting on a hot day. Nearby are some partially-ruined WATERMILLS and abandoned houses, hidden among lush vegetation. The hillsides are terraced, but only partly cultivated. This hamlet, **Caldeira de Cima**, was abandoned years ago (as were some others on the island), because it was too isolated.

Cross the bridge and continue on the trail, soon crossing another STREAM. Ignore the path off to the left by a FOUNTAIN in front of a BAMBOO GROVE and head straight on along the descending trail.

FAJÃS

Fajãs are small coastal plains that lie at the bottom of sheer cliffs. They come about when great landslides occur and enormous masses of rock fall into the sea (e.g. Fajã do Santo Cristo) or when lava flows into the sea during a volcanic eruption (e.g. Fajã do Ouvidor).

Interrupting the otherwise steep coastline, they are at their most spectacular on São Jorge. Tiny hamlets snuggle on these *fajãs*, where tropical fruits and vegetables are grown. On some of these coastal flats there is even a small brackish lake or lagoon.

Connected only by footpaths with the rest of the island, most of these hamlets were abandoned in the 1980s, but recently some of them are being revitalised by the construction of new roads. Some houses have been renovated and are now used as holiday homes or are even permanently inhabited.

Above: Fajã da Caldeira de Santo Cristo, with its seaside lake

Soon it bends to the left, to reveal — quite unexpectedly — a captivating view out over the first *fajã*, with its hamlet and the lake behind it. The trail now descends the hillside and you pass the first inhabited houses in **Fajã da Caldeira de Santo Cristo**.

Continue straight on along the grassy main trail, between stone walls overgrown by aloes. Turn right at a FOUNTAIN WITH A WATER TAP and pass some old houses to reach the CHURCH (**2h10min**). The side entrance is usually open. The interior is very well kept, with an old baroque pulpit. If the church is closed, you can get the key in one of the nearby houses. From the bell tower, you overlook the idyllic hamlet, set against a backdrop of sheer cliffs rising up to 800m/2625ft.

Follow the track behind the church (from the side entrance) past some houses, then take the first turn on your left. This track rises past a house on your right with a bar/restaurant ('O BORGES') and an old wine press inside. Turn right at a fork. Soon the old walled-in cemetery is seen up on your left. The wires hanging down from the cliffs were once used to lower firewood and animal fodder down to the coast. Pass below a steep and dark rock face and skirt the LAKE by the shore. Then you pass the few partly-abandoned houses of **Fajã dos Tijolos** ('Fajã of the Tiles').

Not far beyond a high (seasonal) waterfall up to the left, you reach **Fajã do Belo** ('Fajã of the Beautiful'; **2h50min**). Here, too, most of the houses have been abandoned and are partly in ruins. The trail undulates along the hillside, passing another waterfall (**Ribeira do Ferro**). Eventually you can see your destination, **Fajã dos Cubres**, with its hamlet and lake.

The trail snakes downhill and continues on this *fajã* as a gravel road. The gravel road takes you direct to the CHURCH (**3h40min**), where your pre-arranged taxi should be waiting at the BAR opposite.

Loural • Fajã de Além • Fajã de São João • São Tomé

Distance/time: 9km/5.6mi; 3h20min

Grade: moderate. The walk begins with a steady descent of 500m/1640ft down to the coast. Then it undulates along the coastline before finally climbing over 400m/1310ft. At Loural you may encounter low cloud, but this usually clears when you descend.

Equipment: see pages 47-48; optional: bathing things

How to get there: by 🚗 taxi or with friends from Velas (40km) to the church at Loural. (Access by bus is not practicable at present because of the inconvenient times.) The driver should follow the main road (EN2) from Velas towards Topo. Some 9km beyond the right-hand turning to Ribeira Seca, there is a small building on the left-hand side of the road ('SRHE 1998'). Opposite it, the road signposted to 'Lourais' (plural of Loural) turns right over a bridge and leads to the village church. The taxi drivers usually know the spot if you tell them that you want to walk from Loural to São Tomé via Fajã de São João.
To return: by 🚗 same private transport back to Velas (45km). Arrange in advance to be picked up at the church at São Tomé. On your return, you could take a short detour to Manadas, to visit the church of Santa Bárbara, the most beautiful baroque church in the Azores.

Short walk: Loural — Fajã de São João (5km/3mi; 1h20min). Moderate; equipment and access as above. Follow the main walk to the small church at Fajã de São João; arrange in advance to be picked up there.

This captivating walk is a counterpart to Walk 20, but this route takes you along the steep south coast. Cliffs covered by lush vegetation, idyllic hamlets, a gorgeous valley with a running stream and far-reaching views across the sea to the neighbouring island of Pico await you. This hike is a 'must' for any serious walker!

Start out by turning left at the wide junction opposite the CHURCH in **Loural 2°**. On reaching a fork in the road, bear right downhill.

Serra do Topo, with Pico in the distance

Keep following the road as it winds down past houses and pastures. The road ends at the last house in **Loural 3°** (**15min**).

Continue straight on downhill, passing to the right of the house. Bear left when the track forks almost immediately. The route swings left, down into a lush green ravine, where a waterfall tumbles down the wooded escarpment and splashes into a rock pool. Cross the wild and romantic ravine on a bridge and follow the track through dense woodland. The wires hanging over the treetops are used by the locals to bring tree heather branches down from the hills, so they can use it as firewood.

Eventually the trees open up, affording a first view of the coast. You pass old terraced fields and occasional stone houses, mostly dilapidated, belonging to the abandoned hamlet of **Fajã de Além**. The track swings right before bending back left at a SMALL STONE HOUSE which is still inhabited. Keep following the main track. A hollow opens up in a rock on the left; overgrown by a huge fig tree, it serves as an animal pen. The terraced fields are very fertile and enjoy a lot of sunshine. Vines, beans, melons, bananas — almost everything thrives here.

Close to the coastline, the track crosses a bridge over the **Ribeira de São João** (**1h05min**). The river cascades down through a ravine, where yams are grown on small terraced fields. The rock pools by the bridge are most inviting for a refreshing dip, and you can take a rest in the shade of the bridge. Some old watermills can be seen beside the track and nearby.

Beyond the bridge the track leads into a hamlet with beautiful old stone houses. There is a slipway for the fishing boats on the coast to the right. Continue ahead on the cobbled track, to reach the small CHURCH at **Fajã de São João** (**1h20min**), *where the Short walk ends.* There is a bar on your right with a big dragon tree beside it; the access road to this hamlet comes down on the left.

Continue ahead on the village street. Past the last inhabited house, the track winds uphill through fertile but partly-abandoned terraced fields. Just before the track ends you reach a small group of houses, with a WATER TAP at a building (**Saramagueira; 1h40min**).

Climb the stone steps beside the water tap, heading uphill past an inhabited house. The path is somewhat overgrown; initially it rises slightly to the right, before bending to the left and continuing

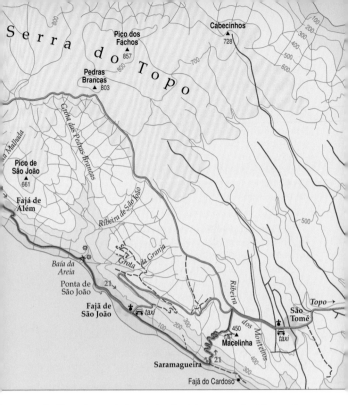

to ascend. Then the path bends back right, now climbing rather steeply in zigzags as an old, partly-cobbled trail. The continuous ascent on the wooded escarpment is quite strenuous, but the gradient eases when terraced fields open up on your left.

You reach a field track at the EDGE OF THE CLIFFS (**3h10min**). Rolling pastureland runs inland, and you can see the clock tower of São Tomé's church some distance away. If you're not pressed for time, you could follow this field track a short way to the right and sit down somewhere on the grass, to enjoy the marvellous view from the cliff edge (some 400m/1300ft above sea level) across the sea to the neighbouring island of Pico. To end the walk, follow the field track to the left, to the main road. Turn right; there is a mini-mercado (not easily recognised from the outside) in the first house on your left. Soon you reach the church of **São Tomé** (**3h20min**).

WALK 22 (PICO 1)

Furna de Frei Matias • Quinta das Rosas • Madalena

Distance/time: 9.8km/6.1mi; 2h20min

Grade: easy; a gentle descent from 700m/2300ft down to sea level on good tracks

Equipment: see pages 47-48; optional: bathing things

How to get there: by 🚕 taxi or with friends to the Furna de Frei Matias (9.5km from Madalena); alight on the main road, where a yellow signpost points right, along a gravel track (all taxi drivers know this spot).
To return: the walk ends in Madalena

Opening hours
Museu dos Vinhos do Pico: Tue-Fri 09.00-12.30, 14.00-17.30; Sat/Sun 09.00-12.30

Old tracks are followed on parts of this walk, which takes you down the northwestern slopes of Pico and into Madalena. This excursion is easily arranged as a day-trip from Faial, and the good

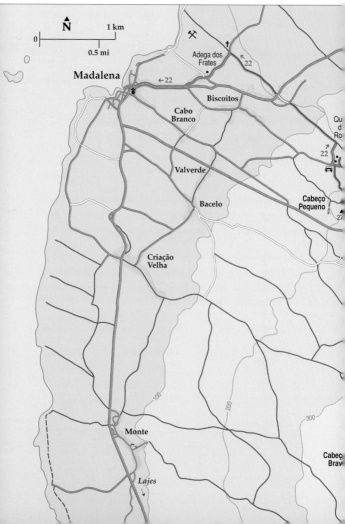

news for late risers is that you don't even have to take the early-morning boat, as you have plenty of time. From an impressive lava tunnel, you stroll downhill through undulating pastureland and a park-like landscape with orchards and coppices. As you approach Madalena, you encounter huge truncated piles of stones in the fields: these *maroiços* almost look like prehistoric monuments, but they are just heaped-up volcanic stones where the land had to be cleared before it could be cultivated. On your way down, you can picnic at the Quinta das Rosas, a former manor house with a fine garden. Near the end of the walk, you pass through vineyards hidden behind high drystone walls, before reaching Madalena, where you can visit the wine museum located in the 17th-century Carmelite convent.

Start out at the **Furna de Frei Matias** ('Brother Matthew's Cavern'). This long vault-like gallery was formed by a lava tunnel

(see page 89). Access to this green and mossy underground cavern is possible through two openings. To reach the *furna* from the main road, follow the SIGNPOSTED GRAVEL TRACK past the iron gate. Pass a CATTLE TROUGH on the left just beyond it and continue ahead, to climb some steps. Turn right in front of the stone wall and go round a small hump, to find the middle opening.

After exploring the cave, return to the main road and walk back towards Madalena. Ignore the first gravel track off to the right and continue on the main road as it curves to the left. Soon after the curve, tracks turn off on either side of the road. Leave the road here and turn right down the track, descending between low stone walls. Enjoy fine views over undulating pastureland and across the Canal do Faial to the island of Faial rising beyond the strait. As revealed by some openings in the ground, more lava tunnels hide in the surrounding fields.

Meet the MAIN ROAD again (**30min**) and cross it, to continue straight ahead on your downhill track. When you meet another ASPHALT ROAD (**45min**), head a few paces to the right, then turn left downhill immediately on a gravel track, surrounded by meadows, coppices and orchards with citrus and apple trees. Come to yet another ASPHALT ROAD (**1h10min**) and follow it to the right. When you reach the main road a few minutes later, turn left for some 75m/yds, until you can turn right on a gravel track; now the first big heap of piled-up stones is seen on the right.

The field track winds between low stone walls through rolling countryside; most of the fields around here have been cleared of volcanic rocks. The wooded brow of **Cabeço Grande** rises to your right, while **Cabeço Pequeno** is seen on the left. Ignore a minor

Pyramid at the Quinta das Rosas, setting for Picnic 20. The neighbouring island of Faial rises to the left, in the distance.

track turning off right. Soon reach a fork in the track where you turn right. (At this fork, the transmitter mast seen previously comes into view again on your left, just above the right flank of Cabeço Pequeno.) Meet an asphalt road (**1h 30min**) opposite the **Quinta das Rosas** ('Centro Apicola'). A few paces to the right is the entrance to the picnic area which has been lovingly laid out in the *quinta* gardens (Picnic 20).

To continue the walk, follow the asphalt road a few metres/yards downhill, then turn right on a tarred lane at the entrance to the Centro Apicola, passing a small TRANSFORMER BUILDING almost immediately. Continue alongside the perimeter wall of the garden. At the end of the garden boundary, where the wall ends, there is a small parking area. Follow the gravel track to the left here, descending through cultivated fields and fertile orchards. Keep ahead on the main track, ignoring all side tracks, until you meet a wide TARRED ROAD (**1h55min**). Cross it and continue ahead on the gravel road; the fire brigade building is to the right.

Soon, on the outskirts of Madalena, cross another road lined by some houses and bear left downhill on a slightly overgrown gravel track, passing to the left of a house. This track runs between high drystone walls hiding well-tended vineyards behind them. You can also see abandoned fields overgrown by trees and bushes, with crumbling stone walls in the shady undergrowth. Meet an asphalt road in front of a Norfolk pine *(Araucaria);* to the right there is a SHRINE WITH BENCHES in the middle of the road (**2h10min**).

Turn left and follow the road past villas; they mostly belong to former emigrants who have returned to their island. Turn right at the road junction by an electricity PYLON WITH A TRANSFORMER. On your right there is a fine estate flanked by a New Zealand Christmas tree *(Metrosiderus excelsa)* at the entrance, the old ADEGA DOS FRATES ('The Lay Brothers' Wine Cellar'). This monastic vineyard, once belonging to the Carmelites, has been turned into a wine museum; the building on the right houses the old distillery. Above the walled vineyards there is an extraordinary grove of dragon trees with a particularly fine specimen — the largest and oldest dragon tree in the Azores.

Turn left at the fork in the road with another Norfolk pine in its middle. Soon meet the cobbled main road lined by plane trees and follow it right into **Madalena** (**2h20min**).

WALK 23 (PICO 2)

The ascent of Pico

Distance/time: 7km/4.3mi to the rim of the crater (Pico Grande) and back (ascent 2h30min, descent 2h); 8.5km/ 5.3mi up to the summit (Piquinho) and back (ascent 3h30min, descent 2h30min)

Grade: difficult, with a generally steep ascent of over 1000m/3280ft, partly over loose stones and scree. Good physical condition, sufficient acclimatisation and mountaineering experience are essential prerequisites for this climb. For the ascent of Piquinho, you should be sure-footed and have a head for heights. After a number of accidents, some of them fatal, *it is required that you climb Pico with a guide* who knows the weather patterns and the route. Guides can be hired through the local tourist office, taxi drivers and some hotels. For security reasons you have to register with the *bombeiros voluntários* (fire brigade) in Madalena before you make the climb; the guides and taxi drivers all know about this. A recommended local guide and taxi driver who speaks excellent English is João Xavier, tel: 962 408417, e-mail joaomadtaxi@clix.pt

Equipment: see pages 47-48; *do* take warm clothing as well, and binoculars, if you have them.

How to get there and return: only by 🚗 taxi or car; 18km from Madalena. Drive along the main EN3 road, heading towards the interior of the island. Some 10km beyond Madalena you pass the right turn to the Furna de Frei Matias (Walk 23). Continue along the main road for another 3km and then turn right on an asphalt road (the 'Casa do Abrigo' is at the junction). After about 5km along this road you reach a parking area with an information board near the Cabeço das Cabras; the ascent begins here.

Special note: — Don't confuse two distant caves: the 'Furna de Frei Matias' (Walk 23) is passed by car along the main road, whereas the 'Furna' is reached

Rising steeply to 2351m/7711ft, Pico is the highest mountain in the Azores and in the whole of Portugal — a huge peak that is among the most beautiful volcanoes in the world. Its ascent rewards the hiker with a magnificent panorama over all the other islands of the central group. The main crater (Pico Grande) at the top of the mountain has a diameter of 500 metres (just under half a mile); there is a sheer drop of about 30m/100ft down into it. The summit itself (Piquino) is a volcanic cone that rises another 100m/330ft above the eastern rim of the crater.

On the climb to the summit of Pico

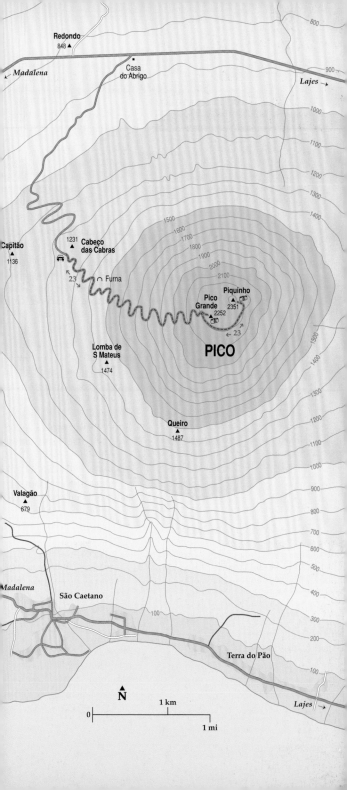

WALLED VINEYARDS

A testimony to the arduous work of generations who cleared the stony land, the ubiquitous enclosures on the western coast of Pico form a unique pattern of cultivation. The stones are piled up into countless drystone walls encircling tiny vineyards. These enclosures protect the vines from the wind, thus helping the grapes to ripen and prevent bruising. A large area of Pico's walled vineyards is now protected as a UNESCO World Heritage Site.

Wine-growing was introduced on Pico in the 16th century by Catholic Orders who planted the first vines. They lived in Horta on Faial, from where the managed their estates on Pico. The *verdelho* white wine from Pico gained a high reputation and was exported to Europe. It was even sent to Russia, where it was appreciated by the Tsar.

Many vines died from mildew in 1852. About 20 years later, just when the vines had been replanted, they were destroyed once again, this time by phylloxera, an American parasite that was to kill most European vines. On Pico, people did not go to the trouble of grafting on American varieties resistant to phylloxera, but started making wine from the American vines. The fragrant, but slightly sharp and astringent aroma gave the wine its name — *vinho de cheiro* ('wine of fragrance').

This red wine is still produced in many private *adegas* as a house wine. The subsequent introduction of new grape varieties has resulted in fine table wines, for instance the red Basalto and the white Terras de Lava. A visit to Pico will not be complete, however, without tasting the rough *vinho de cheiro* — just ask for a jug of local red wine or the bottled Cavaco in a bar or restaurant.

Photograph: walled vineyards on Terceira

The ascent begins at an altitude of 1220m/4000ft, near the **Cabeço das Cabras** ('Goats' Peak'). You follow a path that starts at the parking area, rising across slopes covered with heather and thyme, to the **Furna**, a cavern inside a volcanic cone (**25min**). From here the ascent continues on the path, soon coming to the first of the 1.5m/5ft-high CONCRETE POSTS (**45min**) that mark the steep climb up to the crater rim. They are placed at intervals of about 100m/yds but, unfortunately, some have been damaged and are hard to see in thick cloud.

The final posts are found close to the RIM OF THE CRATER (**Pico Grande**; **2h30min**). Bear round to the right, as there is a sheer drop from the rim down into the crater *(take care!)*. You enjoy a magnificent view down into the main crater with its inner peak (Piquinho) and the panorama over the neighbouring islands floating on an azure ocean.

If you intend to climb the steeply rising rock summit, you will follow the declining rim of the crater in an anti-clockwise direction until you reach the crater floor, then scramble up the rock to the SUMMIT of **Piquinho** (also called Ponta do Pico; **3h30min**). The return is via the same route (**6h**).

WALK 24 (FAIAL 1)

Horta • Alto da Cruz • Praia do Almoxarife

Distance/time: 11.4km/7.1mi; 4h

Grade: easy, with ascents totalling 340m/1115ft on good tracks and roads

Equipment: see pages 47-48; optional: bathing things

How to get there: the walk starts in Horta

To return: by 🚐 from Praia do Almoxarife back to Horta; journey time 25min

This pleasant walk starts with a leisurely stroll through Horta before following old cobbled roads and field tracks through the countryside to Praia do Almoxarife. A magnificent sandy bay facing the neighbouring island of Pico is waiting for you — ideal for a refreshing dip. You can end the day in one of the restaurants where fresh fish is served.

Referring to the plan of Horta on page 43, **start out** at PETER'S CAFÉ SPORT above the HARBOUR. Follow the esplanade north past the tourist information office, **Turismo** [1] and the Estalagem de Santa Cruz, a hotel that is housed in the old Castelo de Santa Cruz. Reach the **Praça do Infante** [2], a public garden on the right with a memorial to Henry the Navigator. From here you have a nice view of the famous marina, legendary meeting-point of all skippers on the cross-Atlantic route. Continue ahead on RUA CONSELHEIRO MEDEIROS (also called Rua Direita), passing to the left of the CAFÉ INTERNACIONAL. Soon the imposing **Igreja de São Francisco** [3] rises on your left; here you go up the RAMPA DE SÃO FRANCISCO.

Turn left round the church and continue uphill. Further up the hillside you can see the pretty buildings of the former German Cable Company, now housing government offices. Turn right into RUA MARCELINO LIMA at the T-junction and go past the **Assembleia Legislativa Regional dos Açores** [5], the Regional Parliament of the Azores. Pass the Hotel Horta and bear right down RUA MEDICO AVELAR. Turn right downhill on RUA E SULCÃO in front of an *império* (see page 39), now enjoying a splendid view of Pico.

Turn left at the next T-junction, now once again on RUA DIREITA. You reach the huge main church, the **Igreja Matriz de São Salvador** [6] almost immediately. This baroque church dates from the former Jesuit college and boasts a magnificent interior with splendid decoration and furnishings. The old monastic complex now houses the interesting MUNICIPAL MUSEUM [7]. Note the earthen model of the island in the small public garden below the church. Continue ahead on RUA ERNESTO REBELO, passing to the left of the POST OFFICE [8]. Soon the imposing Art Deco building of the Sociedade Amor da Patria is seen on your left, decorated with hydrangea ornaments; dragon trees flank the entrance. This patriotic club ('Love of the Fatherland Society') is somewhat comparable to a Freemasons' lodge.

Pass to the right of a chapel commemorating a volcanic eruption near Praia do Norte in 1672, to reach the pretty **Praça da República** [9] with its typical Azorean bandstand. (The walled-in MARKET [10]

115

It has become a tradition that all transatlantic skippers arriving in Horta commemorate their journey by painting a picture on the harbour mole (below). Sometimes tears are shed when the sailors depart ... but 'only for you' (top).

is on the right-hand side.) Continue ahead past honey locust trees with incredibly thorny trunks, and follow the wide street with palm trees in the middle. At the end of the street, turn right for a few paces, then go left almost immediately, into RUA DA CONCEIÇÃO. Soon you cross the **Ribeira de Flamengos** and reach a SQUARE (**1h**) with an Art Deco church in the middle, the **Igreja da Conceição** [11].

Now referring to the map opposite, walk past the left side of the church and continue straight ahead on a road ascending between houses. Almost immediately, keep left on an old cobbled 'highway' (literally), running parallel with the road below. After a few minutes it rejoins the road near some old *quintas*. Continue uphill on the road, soon passing under an OLD ARCH. Just past it, ignore a sharp turn to the right. Flanked by tall stone walls, the road (CALÇADA DA CONCEIÇÃO) now rises. Not far beyond a ROAD BRIDGE crossing overhead, you reach a wide road junction where there is another *império* and a BUS SHELTER (**1h25min**). Bear diagonally right uphill on the cobbled road. Soon ignore a right turn towards Praia do Almoxarife and keep on the cobbled road, which bends to the left. A minute later, bear left again at a fork. Ignore the following right turn and continue straight ahead. This quiet road runs along a ridge, with fine views of the Flamengos Valley and Horta to your left and Praia do Almoxarife to the right. Some of the old windmills on this crest have been renovated.

Pass the **Império da Estrada da Caldeira** and then a TRANSMITTER, both on your left. Leave the road a short time later when you reach a fork by a pretty old VILLA (**2h**); its archway is decorated with *azulejos* (glazed tiles) from 1901 in the Flemish style. Bear right up the 'CAMINHO VELHO' here. This tarred lane climbs past some houses before it continues as a field track. Shortly after passing an old RUINED WINDMILL on the right (nothing remains except its stone base), you reach a track junction at a WATERWORKS ('CMH 1988'; **2h 25min**). Turn right here (below an unsightly rubbish tip).

The track now descends through woodland. Bear right at a fork, crossing a bridge over the **Ribeira da Praia**, and continue on the tarred RUA DO CHÃO FRIO past some houses. Soon you reach a cross-roads where you turn left uphill. Shortly after passing a small WATER-PUMPING BUILDING on your left, turn right on a field track. Wild hydrangeas and montbretias grow by the wayside. Bear left at a fork. Soon the track forks again; this time you continue straight ahead and then downhill.

The field track meets a small asphalt road by a BRIDGE; turn right uphill (**3h05min**). Leave the road at the top of the rise and turn left on a reddish crossing track. Soon you see the stone base of an old RUINED WINDMILL on your left. The track runs along the crest of the ridge. Pedro Miguel is the village down in the valley to the left; Pico rises ahead of you, across the strait. When you reach a TRIG POINT on your right (**Alto da Cruz; 3h30min**), there is a good view across the Ribeira da Praia to the opposite ridge with its windmills.

The track now gains a tarred surface and continues to descend. You can already see the sandy beach of Praia do Almoxarife and the church down on the coast. Go left down to the main road in front of a house and follow it a few paces to the right, then turn left up a field track that is cobbled at the outset. There is another RUINED WINDMILL on the rise to your left. Pass a concrete building and follow the grassy field track as it swings left, then right downhill. Now you descend quite steeply between tall Spanish reeds *(Arundo donax)*.

Turn right when the track meets an asphalt road. Turn left down ROCHA VERMELHA DE BAIXO at the next fork. Beyond some houses, you reach the central square (LARGO COLONEL SILVA LEAL) in **Praia do Almoxarife** ('The Shopkeeper's Beach'; **4h**). The eponymous sandy beach that begins here (Picnic 21) is one of the finest in the Azores, affording a splendid view across the strait to Pico. There are several bars and restaurants where you can get refreshments. The BUS SHELTER for your return is in the central square.

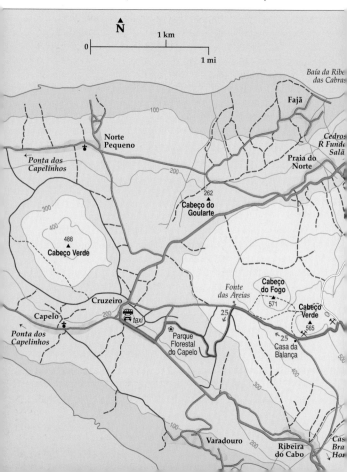

WALK 25 (FAIAL 2)

Caldeira • Cabeço Gordo • Cabeço do Trinta • Parque Florestal • Cruzeiro (Capelo)

Distance/time: 16km/10mi; 4h25min
Grade: moderate. Initially there is a short but fairly steep ascent of 140m/460ft to the highest peak on the island, Cabeço Gordo, followed by a gradual descent along tracks and a road. There is also some level walking alongside a contouring water channel (levada)..

Equipment: see pages 47-48
How to get there: 🚕 taxi or with friends to the parking area at the tunnel entrance to the caldeira, 17km from Horta .
To return: 🚐 or 🚕 pre-arranged taxi from the road junction at Cruzeiro, part of the village of Capelo.
Photograph: Faial's Caldeira

This walk starts out on the rim of the Caldeira (Faial's main crater), where you climb the island's highest peak. The view into the wild and often misty cauldron is a truly spectacular sight. The basin, some 300m/1000ft below, has a marshy floor today, but before the Capelinhos volcano erupted in 1957/58 there was a lake at the bottom. Its water leaked through fissures in the ground when the whole island was shaken by the volcanic upheaval. Leaving the crater's rim, you cross its western slopes, gently descending through pastures and woodland to Cruzeiro — on one section beside a pleasant *levada* (water channel). On your return, you could ask your taxi driver to detour to Ponta dos Capelinhos; see Car tour 5.

Start out from the PARKING PLACE, where a short pedestrian TUNNEL leads to a viewpoint into the crater. Climb up the steps to the left of the tunnel entrance and continue through a GATE on the path to the left; this runs along the RIM of the **Caldeira** towards the highest

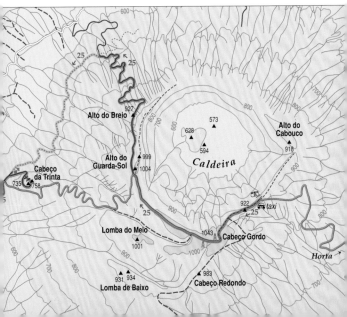

peak, where there is a transmitter. After a few minutes you come to the FIRST TRIG POINT ('IPCC 1997'). Shortly afterwards, you begin the short but fairly steep ascent on a stepped path up to the transmitter on **Cabeço Gordo** ('Bold Peak'; 1043m/3421ft; **30min**).

From the transmitter follow the tarmac road, soon crossing a cattle grid by another small fenced-in transmitter to the left. Leave the road when it bends to the left, turning right on a GRAVEL TRACK (**55min**). This track eventually swings left (**1h10min**) and then winds down through Japanese cedars (*Cryptomerias*). Watch for a water channel passing under the track (at an altitude of 650m/2130ft). Leave the track here and turn left along this *levada* (**1h45min**).

Soon the *levada* bridges a ravine. Keep on the *levada* path until you reach a large open WATER TANK (**2h15min**). Pass to the right of it and go up the gravel track just afterwards. Soon take a sharp left turn (the walk will later continue ahead from this junction). The track rises and soon bends to the right. Leave it almost immediately and climb a path to the left; it takes you through a TUNNEL into the crater of **Cabeço do Trinta** ('Summit of the Thirty'; **2h20min**). This is an impressive, if somewhat spooky, spot — the figure '30' is a synonym for the devil. A few decades ago there were plans to use the crater as a water reservoir, but the volcanic rock was too porous.

Climb the path inside the crater; then, from the rim, follow the track to the right, passing the fork where you originally came from the water tank. Continue ahead for less then 100m/yds, to meet a tarmac road on a bend. Follow it down to the right and stay with this road as it winds downhill, ignoring a gravel track off right (**3h**) and a wide right turn to Praia do Norte in front of a QUARRY. Pass another big QUARRY on the flanks of the volcanic cone of **Cabeço Verde** to your right. After 200m/yds you reach a junction with a small house in the middle, the **Casa da Balança** ('House of Scales'; **3h20min**).

Bear right to continue down the road, then turn left opposite a dilapidated WASHHOUSE at the **Fonte das Areias** (**3h35min**), descending a stony track into woodland. Bear right at the fork reached after just two minutes. Keep downhill along this gravel track flanked by ginger lilies until you reach another fork where you turn right (**3h50min**). Almost immediately, at the next fork, bear right again. Climb slightly for a few minutes, to a wide T-junction next to some huge tree trunks. Bear left and follow this woodland track straight ahead. A short time later, continue ahead on a tarred road through the **Parque Florestal do Capelo** (**4h10min**), past the barbecues and toilets. Turn left at a T-junction in front of a typical Azorean farmstead (museum).

On meeting the main road, turn right and follow it past houses (there is a handicraft centre on the left with interesting photos of the 1957/8 eruption) to the road junction in **Cruzeiro** (part of the village of **Capelo**; **4h25min**), where you will find a bar/minimercado and a BUS STOP.

WALK 26 (FLORES 1)

Ponta Ruiva • Cedros • Porto da Lagoa • Parque Florestal da Fazenda • Santa Cruz

Distance/time: 14.1km/8.8mi; 5h

Grade: moderate to difficult. Several valleys are crossed on steep trails that can be slippery after rain. Some streams have to be crossed on stones. Overall ascent of 540m/1770ft

Equipment: see pages 47-48

How to get there: 🚕 taxi to Ponta Ruiva. Turn right down the village street at the T-junction by a bus shelter, soon passing an electricity sub-station. Then the road swings left uphill before bending right. The old trail down to Fajã da Ponta Ruiva turns off left on this right bend. Almost immediately, before the road begins to rise more steeply, the footpath to Cedros turns off, also on the left. Most taxi drivers know the place.
To return: The walk ends in Santa Cruz, where there is a taxi rank.

The ups and downs of this 'roller-coaster' walk take you across wild valleys and up wooded hillsides. You also follow a pleasant watercourse *(levada)* to a reservoir, before passing a beautiful picnic area. The final stretch takes you all the way to Santa Cruz.

Start out in the village of **Ponta Ruiva** ('Red Point') by descending the old trail; almost immediately there is a splendid view into the wooded valley of the Ribeira Funda. Keep left downhill when you reach a fork in a few minutes. Soon you pass a WATER TANK on the right. When you reach another fork almost immediately, this time bear right on the trail that contours along the hillside. The old terraced fields, with their hedgerows of Victorian laurel serving as windbreaks, are mostly abandoned. Cross a small concrete BRIDGE over a stream at the head of the valley and bear left at the fork that follows almost immediately. Soon cross another small concrete bridge over the main stream, the **Ribeira Funda** (**15min**).

The trail now rises through woodland on the other side of the valley and eventually passes a rock face. Turn right when you meet a T-JUNCTION a short time later (**50min**). Quickly leaving the trees behind, you walk between walled pastures lined by hydrangeas. After crossing a small stream (**Ribeira das Lajes**), you pass two old MILLS by the **Ribeira da Privada**; the old millstone is displayed outside the building. Continue ahead on the road when you reach the CEMETERY, soon passing the church of **Cedros** on your right (**1h10min**).

Go straight across the main road and continue past the bus shelter along the village street lined by houses. Bear left downhill

The terraced east coast near Ponta Ruiva, with Corvo in the distance

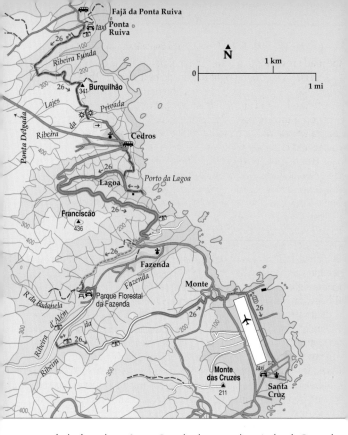

at a fork; from here Santa Cruz looks very close indeed. Cross the main road again and continue straight down the grassy trail. A steep descent follows, on an old cobbled trail with stone steps in the middle. High stone walls flank the trail when it enters the woods. Join a track near a house and continue to descend. Soon you meet an asphalt road, where you turn sharp left downhill for a detour to the coast. At the end of the road, follow the old cobbled trail down into the valley and across the old BRIDGE. Continue on the other side of the valley, past a WATER-PUMPING BUILDING. The trail takes you down to the secluded stony bay of **Porto da Lagoa** (1h35min). Some rocks from an eroded volcano that has almost completely disappeared rise from the sea off the coast here.

Return the same way across the bridge; then keep ahead on the road, passing the fork where you came down earlier. Bananas and yams are cultivated on terraced fields in this fertile valley. When you eventually meet the main road, turn left across the BRIDGE (**2h20min**) and follow the road for the next two kilometres. After a bend, there is a sweeping view out over the village of Fazenda in a valley, with the church perched on a hill above the houses.

Now *watch out* for the turn-off where you have to leave the road. This comes about 30m/yds beyond the **Fazenda** village sign, where the road crosses over a water channel (levada). Go through the GAP IN THE LOW WALL on the right-hand side of the road (**2h45min**) and follow the water channel inland on the narrow path that runs along its left-hand side. This path is somewhat overgrown.

Soon a track crosses the path, quickly followed by a concrete levada BRIDGE with a handrail on the left. Cross the bridge over a ravine and continue to hug the levada on the tree-lined path, until you reach a sheer drop. Although this short section could be traversed, it is best to cross the levada on a concrete slab just before this drop and recross it on the next concrete slab just round the bend. You pass a small stone house on the right and later go over a crossing water channel. Continue as far as the end of an open space, where the levada has four concrete slabs forming a FOOT-BRIDGE. Leave the path here (the way ahead is overgrown) and bear left on a fainter path leading down to the RIVER BED. Cross on boulders and follow the track up the far side, to a road. A few paces to the right is the wall of the RESERVOIR at the confluence of the **Ribeira da Badanela** and the **Ribeira d'Além** (**3h10min**).

Turn left along the road. It leads up to the **Parque Florestal da Fazenda** (**3h15min**), an attractive picnic area. Continue up the road for another two minutes, before turning sharp right. Follow this road up past houses for about 150m/yds, then bear left at the fork, up a gravel road lined by street lamps. Pass a house on the left. As you climb, a beautiful view opens up on your right over a wide valley, framed by high mountains — a panorama somewhat reminiscent of the Alps.

After passing an enclosure with a CATTLE TROUGH on your left (**3h40min**), watch for the turn-off where you have to leave the road. When the gradient eases some 150m/yds past the enclosure, turn left down a footpath (easily missed, as it is somewhat concealed by foliage). It descends as a sunken trail (cobbled in parts) through woodland. Cross the **Ribeira da Fazenda** (**3h45min**) on stones. On the far side, the old trail rises again; it is now lined by hydrangeas and junipers. Soon there is a beautiful view of Fazenda.

Reaching a turning area, continue ahead on the concreted track. At the top of the rise, Santa Cruz comes into view. Ignore turn-offs left and right, but turn right when you meet a ROAD JUNCTION near the first houses (**4h30min**). Fork sharp left after just 50m/yds, then turn right down another road almost immediately. Turn right again at the following T-junction. Join the main road and go down a few paces to the right before taking the left turn ('OP 1937'). Follow this lane downhill; the old whaling factory is ahead of you on the coast.

Descend a flight of steps past some houses. When you reach the bottom of the hill, continue ahead on a road past the end of the AIRSTRIP. Turn right at the fork in front of a FOUNTAIN (**4h45min**). Now carry straight on until you can turn right at the crossroads by the POST OFFICE. Soon you reach the main square (PRAÇA MARQUES DE POMBAL) in **Santa Cruz** (**5h**), where there is a TAXI RANK.

WALK 27 (FLORES 2)

Lajes • Parque de Lazer • Fajã de Lopo Vaz • Parque de Lazer • Porto das Lajes

Distance/time: 10.4km/6.5mi; 2h20min

Grade: moderate. Steep cliff path down to the beach and back up, with a height difference of 200m/655ft. The return to Lajes is by road.

Equipment: see pages 47-48; optional: bathing things

How to get there: 🚌 taxi to 'Morros', a crossroads in the upper part of Lajes, where there is a signpost to the Fajã de Lopo Vaz (19km from Santa Cruz). *Note:* there are *two* signposted turn-offs from the main road; you want the *lower* one (where there is an *império* just opposite); most taxi drivers know the place.
To return: 🚌 taxi from Lajes back to Santa Cruz (18km). If you pre-arrange your transport, a good meeting-point is the car park above the harbour.

Short walk: Parque de Lazer — Fajã de Lopo Vaz — Parque de Lazer (2.4km/1.5mi; 1h20min). Grade and equipment as above. Access and return: 🚌 car or taxi to the Parque de Lazer picnic site. Follow the main walk from the 20min-point down to the Fajã de Lopo Vaz and return the same way.

H idden on the south coast of Flores is a secluded bay backed by steep cliffs and fringed by a sand and pebble beach. The old cobbled cliff trail followed in this walk connects this secluded spot with the rest of the island. The *fajã* is said to have a tropical micro-climate, the warmest place on Flores. Fruit is grown on the coastal flats, and you may well meet a local trudging up the trail, laden with bunches of bananas. The name Fajã de Lopo Vaz (like the islet of Maria Vaz off the northwest coast; see Walk 29) presumably dates back some 400 years, when Spanish settlers came to Flores.

Start out at the CROSSROADS in the upper part of **Lajes**, where a village street with a signpost pointing to the Fajã de Lopo Vaz crosses the main road. Follow this street, passing a Holy Ghost chapel dating from 1846 (an *império;* see page 39) on the right and a bandstand on the left almost immediately. Cross the bridge over the **Ribeira do Loureiro**; the old stone bridge can be seen down on the right. Stay ahead on the village street past a FOUNTAIN on the left, but turn left when you meet a T-junction. Soon the road swings left, leaving the last houses behind. The road runs through undulating pastureland, past a wide gravel road off right, and ends at the **Parque de Lazer** picnic site (**20min**), where there is a stone cross (CRUZ DA PEDRA). It was originally erected in 1856 when a new section of path down to the Fajã de Lopo Vaz was opened, but replaced by the present one in 1997.

Go down the old cobbled trail that starts here. Care is needed on the steep descent, which includes well over three hundred steps, as the surface is often uneven and sometimes slippery. Much of the earlier part of the descent has vegetation on both sides of the trail, so it is not vertiginous. Soon you can see a STATUE OF THE VIRGIN tucked into the rock on your right. The first *fajã* that comes into view is Quebrada Nova (da Costa do Lajedo) in the background, a rather recent cliff collapse at Rocha Alta that occurred in 1980. The descent eases as the path contours along terraced fields which are

*Top: harvesting bananas; below:
Rocha dos Bordões (near Walk 28)*

mostly abandoned. You reach the **Fajã de Lopo Vaz** (**50min**) near a summer cottage. The bay is fringed by a stony beach, backed by a sweep of fine sand. Caution: Don't swim here unless the sea is dead calm; the undertow can be very strong.

Climb back up the way you came and return to the **Parque de Lazer** picnic site (**1h40min**). Continue to the CROSSROADS (**2h**) where you started out and go straight across the main road, down a village street. Soon cross the **Ribeira Seca** and take the second turn on the right (after passing a mini-mercado with some petrol pumps). Continue straight ahead past a right turn, soon recrossing the main road. Pass the village CHURCH in **Lajes** on your right and recross the Ribeira Seca shortly after.

Turn left down the footpath just after the BRIDGE. Cross the wide access road to the harbour and continue down a small concrete footpath between houses. On meeting the wide road again, turn left for a few paces, then descend another footpath. Rejoin the road and follow it downhill to the car park overlooking the **Porto das Lajes** (**2h 20min**). A sign, 'TURISMO/MUSEU BALEEIRO', pointing left, leads you down to a sheltered bay with a sandy beach, with picnic tables and other facilities, including showers.

WALK 28 (FLORES 3)

Lajedo • Mosteiro • Fajãzinha • Fajã Grande • Porto da Fajã Grande

See also photograph page 125
Distance/time: 8.5km/5.3mi; 3h40min
Grade: moderate walk on clear, undulating trails, with ascents totalling 430m/1410ft. There is usually water in the Ribeira Grande, so you have to wade through; the rocks can be quite slippery and there may be a strong current after heavy rain. The trail can be slippery, too, and there are steep sections in places.
Equipment: see p 47-48
How to get there: 🚌 taxi to the church in Lajedo (20km from Santa Cruz through the interior of the island or 25km along the coast road).

To return: meet your pre-arranged taxi at the bar/restaurant at Porto da Fajã Grande (22km back to Santa Cruz).
Short walks: From Lajedo to Mosteiro or Fajãzinha. You can split the walk into several sections, meeting your taxi at the church in Mosteiro (the 1h15min-point; 2.9km/ 1.8mi; an ascent of 180m/ 590ft) or in the square near the church in Fajãzinha (the 2h30min-point; 6.1km/3.8mi; an ascent of 330m/1080ft). Grade, equipment and access as above.
Photograph: detail from the império *in Mosteiro*

The old and partly-cobbled trail followed in this walk connects isolated hamlets above the island's western coast, undulating as it crosses several valleys. All along, there are magnificent views over the dramatic landscape. The walk ends in Fajã Grande, the most westerly European outpost in the North Atlantic.

Start out at the CHURCH in **Lajedo** (literally 'Place with many flagstones', referring to the nearby coast). Go over to the *império* (Holy Ghost chapel; see page 39) and turn right at the road junction in front of it. The road bends left, soon leading out of the village. Leave the road five minutes later, on a sharp left bend: continue straight ahead. You are now following an old cobbled trail that gradually begins to descend. The Rocha dos Bordões, a rocky upthrust with basalt columns that look like the pipes of a giant organ, rises on the right (photograph page 125). After crossing a first stream, the trail is soon flanked by stone walls on both sides.

Your first major stream crossing (**Ribeira da Lapa**; **30min**) is via a small BRIDGE, which you may not even notice. Only if you peer back through the vegetation after crossing it can you just make out two arches of this old stone bridge, said to have been built by the Spanish four hundred years ago. The path now becomes somewhat overgrown. You come to another stream crossing (**Ribeira do Fundão; 45min**), where you have to go a few metres/yards upstream on stepping stones to find the continuation of your route. After this crossing the old cobbled trail climbs steeply. Ignore one or two minor turn-offs. A track takes you to the road into **Mosteiro** ('Monastery'; the name apparently refers to some cliffs at the Cabeço do Sinal, a rocky upthrust once dominating the village, but these rocks have since been quarried and no longer give the impression of a monastery). Turn left and soon arrive at the CHURCH (**1h15min**).

126

Go straight ahead, passing to the right of the CHURCH SQUARE (a small green space with some benches), following the road down towards the sea. Very quickly, leave the road where it bends right and continue straight ahead on a concreted track, passing some old houses. This track crosses a bridge over the **Ribeira do Mosteiro**. The grassy old trail which continues on the far side is still cobbled in places. It rises along the hillside past more old stone houses and rejoins the road. Continue straight ahead and follow this asphalted but little-used road, bending right as you come down the hill into a basin. The road crosses a bridge over the **Ribeira da Caldeira** before curving to the left and rising. At the end of the next right bend, tracks turn off on either side. Take the track on your left and follow it down to a T-junction by a FOUNTAIN WITH WATER TAP. Here you are in the middle of the abandoned and largely ruined hamlet of **Caldeira (1h50min)**; its last inhabitants left in June 1992.

Turn right at this T-junction, then keep left. A steep sunken trail takes you uphill, back to the road, where you continue straight ahead. As you leave Caldeira, the road climbs towards the transmitter mast seen ahead on Cruzeiro da Fajãzinha. Leave the road by forking diagonally left onto the old signposted trail to Fajãzinha, passing a concrete WATER-PUMPING HOUSE almost immediately. On meeting a trail ascending sharply to the right, follow it up to the **Miradouro da Fajãzinha (2h15min)**, from where there is a magnificent view into the lush basin of the Ribeira Grande, with the houses of Fajãzinha spread out far below. Further inland a semicircle of green escarpments rises, with waterfalls dramatically plunging down over perpendicular cliffs. There is a trig point dated 1948 on the rock next to the viewpoint.

Return down the trail to the fork and now bear right, continuing your descent on the wide cobbled trail. A steep descent through woodland takes you down the **Ladeira do Portal** ('Hillside of the Gate'). Join a concreted track when you reach the first houses of **Fajãzinha** near the bottom of the hill, pass the beautiful church of **N S dos Remédios**, built in 1776-1783, and reach the small village SQUARE with trees and benches where you can take a rest **(2h30min)**. There is a welcoming bar in the small shop; note the old safe inside!

Continue onwards from the square by turning left at the ELECTRICITY SUB-STATION, in front of a second shop/bar. Pass a CHAPEL on the right almost immediately. When you reach the last house, the road bends right. Leave it here and follow instead the old trail that descends ahead quite steeply; two old stone houses (WATERMILLS) are on the left. The old trail rejoins the road, where you turn left to continue. Leave the road when it bends left just in front of the river flats overgrown with Spanish reed, and fork right on a path. Now you have to scramble briefly over rocks amidst reed. Some white paint blobs and arrows on the rocks indicate the best way to the river's edge. When you reach the **Ribeira Grande (2h45min)**, look for a suitable crossing place through the boulder-strewn river bed

— either by the pillars of an old bridge that was washed away in 1964 or a little further upstream.

On the far side climb the steep river bank (to the *left* of three white arrows indicating an old, eroded way up). Join the old cobbled trail by a juniper tree. It rises and soon runs close to the cliff edge, but the sheer drop is hidden by vegetation and not vertiginous.* A pleasant stroll now takes you past walled pastures. There is an old whale-watching post on the hill to the left (see page 88).

Eventually you reach the main road into **Fajã Grande**; turn left and follow this cobbled road straight downhill. Pass a small public garden with benches (JARDIM P JOSÉ A CAMÕES). Continue along the village street, passing the Residencial Argonauta on the left and then the CHURCH (**3h 30min**). Now continue straight ahead for ten minutes, to the quay at **Porto da Fajã Grande** (**3h40min**). Take a swim in the sea; the *balneário* at the bar/restaurant, where your taxi driver meets you, has a green space and bathing facilities with showers and toilets.

*At the first fork you could turn right for a detour via the old hamlet of Cuada, now holiday homes; see the map.

WALK 29 (FLORES 4)

Fajã Grande • Ponta da Fajã • Fora da Rocha • Ponta Delgada

See photograph page 18   **Distance/time:** 11.1km/6.9mi; 3h50min

Grade: moderate to difficult, with some steep ascents (430m/1410ft overall).
Do not attempt in low cloud or bad weather when route finding would be very
difficult in the middle section of the walk. Although care is needed on this
stretch, the trail is quite clear most of the time, provided you have good visibility.
After heavy rain the trail will be extremely waterlogged and slippery. None of
the makeshift gates you may have to pass through are mentioned in the text.

Equipment: see pages 47-48

How to get there: 🚌 taxi or with friends to the church in Fajã Grande (23km
from Santa Cruz). Arrange to be collected again at the end of the walk.
To return: a good meeting-point for the return is the supermarket in Ponta
Delgada (20km back to Santa Cruz).

Shorter walk: Fajã Grande — lighthouse/Morro Alto road (7.7km/4.8mi;
2h50min). Grade, equipment and access as above. Follow the main walk to the
2h50min-point and meet your transport on the lighthouse/Morro Alto road.

This is the most popular walk on Flores, affording splendid views
all along — weather permitting! A steep ascent takes you up the
western cliffs of the island, to the isolated plateau with its undulating moorland and pastures. There is a great feeling of solitude
and exhilaration, with sweeping vistas all around as you cross the
uninhabited northwest of Flores. Hydrangeas abound, streams run
cheerfully down the slopes and cows graze on lush pastures.

Start out at the CHURCH in **Fajã Grande**. Go down the cobbled
village street for 100m/yds, then take the first right turn. Soon pass
a *minimercado*. Meet another road, go straight across and continue
ahead on a grassy trail flanked by stone walls. Soon bear right at a
fork. Rejoining the road, cross a bridge over the **Ribeira das Casas**.
Just after, turn right along the river bank for a short detour. An old
footpath takes you upstream past old partly-ruined WATERMILLS to
the **Poço do Bacalhau** ('Codfish Pool'; **15min**). The high waterfall
shown on page 18 plummets down dramatically from the cliffs
overhead into a big rock pool — a spectacular sight after rain.

Return to the road and continue along it for less than 200m/yds,
then fork right on an old trail (concreted at the outset), climbing
between stone walls. You are walking between terraced fields and
garden plots. The old trail rejoins the road; turn right to continue,
soon reaching the first houses of **Ponta da Fajã (45min)**. The
inhabitants of the hamlet were officially forced to leave their homes
after alarming rock falls on 19 December 1987, although most
houses were left untouched by the collapse; the resulting 'wound'
in the escarpment is still clearly visible.

Continue on the track, passing the CHURCH on the right; it soon
becomes an old cobbled trail and bears left at a concreted river
bed. Follow the stony river bed a short way before crossing it, now
climbing on the old grassy trail. Soon this trail begins to mount the
cliffs; it is amply wide and not vertiginous. Little streams cross the
trail, making it muddy and waterlogged in places.

Soon after the trail leads into woodland, you cross another concreted river bed (**Grota do Cavalo**) and reach a fork a short time later (**1h20min**). Bear right uphill on the main trail, soon zigzagging steeply up the wooded cliffs. Pass through a WOODEN GATE (**1h 55min**) on the cliff edge. The gradient now eases, and undulating moorland (**Fora da Rocha**) opens out before you. This is a good spot to pause, with fine views across the steep coastline towards the lighthouse on the Ponta do Albarnaz and over to the neighbouring island of Corvo. The small islet off the coast is Ilhéu de Maria Vaz.

Continue on the main trail which initially heads inland and soon narrows; ignore any minor paths. The route is obvious most of the time, as you cross a succession of valleys and stream beds, surrounded by bushy tree-heather, juniper, spongy mosses and hydrangeas. The first STREAM BED (**2h**) needs to be crossed on boulders; the path continues a few metres/yards upstream.

At a three-way fork, continue on the middle path, ascending between stone walls overgrown by hydrangea hedges. The way becomes less distinct for a short distance over open grassland, but always keep straight ahead. At the end of this section the ground ahead drops away but the path is very clear again. The next distinct section is a sunken trail that has been concreted for a few metres; the stream is diverted in a small channel. Eventually you reach the LIGHTHOUSE/MORRO ALTO ROAD (**2h50min**). *(This is where the Shorter walk ends.)* Turn left on this road and continue downhill.

Leave the road some ten minutes later (**3h**), where the embankment on the right is not stabilised: turn right on the grassy trail down into the valley. The stone cobbles of this old trail are still visible in places. The area beside the **Ribeira do Moinho (3h10min)** is a pleasant picnic spot, with some abandoned WATERMILLS further downstream. The rock pools are perfect for an invigorating dip, with the option of a hydro-massage if you turn your back to the tumbling stream!

To continue the walk, cross the river via the low concrete FOOTBRIDGE. (If there is a heavy water flow you may not be able to cross the bridge because it is awash. In this case you either have to wade through or turn back to the road and continue down to the junction with the lighthouse/Ponta Delgada road. Turn right and follow this road as it swings through the valley of the Ribeira do Moinho, rejoining the main walk at the 3h20min-point. This adds some 15 minutes' walking.)

The path up the far side of the river is quite clear and joins the LIGHTHOUSE/PONTA DELGADA ROAD (**3h 20min**) just past a stone enclosure with an engraving of a man leading a cow and a sign 'JUNTA DA FREGUESIA PONTA DELGADA, FLORES 22-6-90'). Turn right on this road. Ignore both an asphalt road and a gravel road heading right, but keep right when the road forks at a WATER TROUGH (**3h40min**) by the first houses of **Ponta**

Porto
Fajã Gran

Balneário

Fajã
Grande
28

128

Delgada. Cross the main road a few minutes later and continue straight ahead through a small valley on the old village street. Rejoin the main road at an ELECTRICITY SUB-STATION BY A SMALL PUBLIC GARDEN with benches and continue straight ahead past a small CHURCH on the right. Just where the road bends right, there is a SUPER-MARKET on the right (**3h50min**) where your TAXI should be waiting. The street straight ahead leads to the CHURCH.

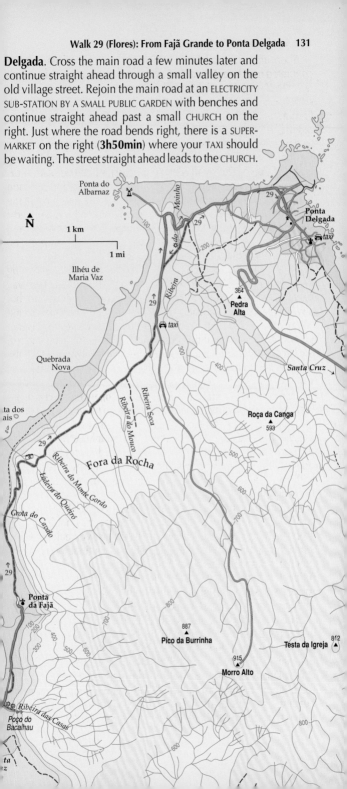

WALK 30 (CORVO)

Vila Nova • Caldeirão • Vila Nova

Distance/time: 11.3km/7mi; 4h15min

Grade: moderate, with a gradual ascent/descent of 550m/1800ft (on roads). The walk is possible even when the crater rim is enveloped in cloud (as it often is!) — you will still catch glimpses into the basin. If you're short of time for the whole walk, take minibus which waits at the harbour up to the top and just walk down.

Equipment: see pages 47-48; waterproof covering for hand luggage during the ferry trip

How to get there and return: 🚢 boat from Santa Cruz or Lajes (Flores) to Corvo; the sailing takes between 45min and 1h30min, depending on the kind of boat and route. During summer, when the sea is calm, a boat usually leaves for Corvo every week. Ask the exact return time when you land on Corvo. For further information and ticket sales, enquire at the harbour in Santa Cruz or Lajes.

Your walk begins at the harbour in **Vila Nova**, the only village on Corvo. It boasts some 400 inhabitants, and all the houses stand closely packed together, to take up the minimum amount of precious soil.

Start out at the HARBOUR by heading for the post office: either follow the main street or walk through a small lane past the church.

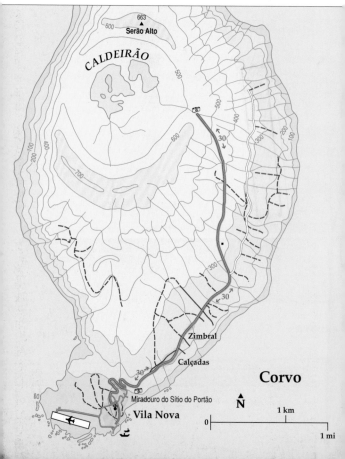

At the POST OFFICE, take the cobbled road that runs uphill. The cobbles end after a bend to the right, and the road becomes asphalted (**20min**). From the **Miradouro do Sítio do Portão (40min)** there is a fine view of Vila Nova nestling around the cove.

Continue to ascend along the road; it begins to lead through an area called **Calçadas** ('Cobbled Trails'; **1h**), where there are traditional houses built with dark drystone walls between the fields. Follow the asphalt road as it bends to the left, at the point where where a gravel road continues straight ahead (**1h30min**). Then you cross a CATTLE GRID and go through a GATE, passing a building on the right (**1h50min**). The road climbs steadily and ends at a viewpoint which affords a fine view into the **Caldeirão**, Corvo's central crater basin (**2h50min**). At its bottom there are small lakes, varying in size according to the rainfall. The slopes opposite have been carefully parcelled out by stone walls. Clouds swirl across the rim of the crater. The setting is one of almost unreal solitude and tranquillity.

Walk back the same way to **Vila Nova (4h15min)**.

Top: Corvo's Caldeirão; below: Corvo from the Flores ferry crossing

BUS AND FERRY TIMETABLES

Listed are all the relevant bus timetables for the walks and picnics described in the book. Note that there are more bus routes. Be sure to check at the relevant tourist information office, to see if any new timetables have been issued. Note that on **Flores** there is a very limited bus service that offers no useful connections for tourists. On **Corvo**, there is usually a bus waiting for the ferry, to take tourists arriving on the island up to the Caldeirão.

SÃO MIGUEL

PONTA DELGADA: *for departure points, see town plan page 28-29*

Ponta Delgada — Mosteiros (via Relva and Varzea); Auto Viação Micaelense; journey time 1h15min
Mon-Fri: 7.50, 10.40, 12.45, 15.00, 16.30, 17.30, 18.50; *Sat:* 7.50, 13.15, 15.00, 17.30, 19.00; *Sun/hols:* 9.00, 12.30, 16.40, 19.45

Mosteiros — Ponta Delgada
Mon-Fri: 6.15, 7.05, 9.05, 12.05, 14.45, 16.35; *Sat:* 6.15, 7.05, 9.05, 12.05, 14.45, 16.35; *Sun/hols:* 7.00, 11.00, 15.15, 18.15

Ponta Delgada — Furnas — Povoação; Varela & Ca.; journey time Ponta Delgada — Furnas 2h, Furnas — Povoação 20min
Mon-Fri: 9.00, 13.45, 16.00, 18.10*, 18.30**; *Sat:* 9.00, 15.00; *Sun/hols:* 9.00, 15.00

Povoação — Furnas — Ponta Delgada
Mon-Fri: 6.30, 8.30, 10.15, 16.00; *Sat:* 11.00, 17.00; *Sun/hols:* 11.00, 17.00
*only Mon-Thur; **only Fri

Ponta Delgada — Ribeira Grande — Furnas; Caetano Raposo & Pereira; journey time Ponta Delgada — Ribeira Grande 35min, Ribeira Grande — Furnas 1h05min
Daily: 7.15, 15.15

Furnas — Ribeira Grande — Ponta Delgada
Daily: 9.10, 17.10

Ponta Delgada — Sete Cidades (via Relva and Varzea); Auto Viação Micaelense; journey time about 1h30min
Mon-Fri: 8.25, 18.25; *Sat:* 15.00; *Sun/hols:* 9.00, 16.10

Sete Cidades — Ponta Delgada (via Relva and Varzea)
Mon-Fri: 7.00, 9.30, 16.25; *Sat:* 7.00, 9.00, 16.25; *Sun/hols:* 10.45, 18.05

Ponta Delgada — João Bom (via Capelas); Auto Viação Micaelense; journey time about 1h25min
Mon-Fri: 9.30, 12.30, 16.00, 18.15, 19.00; *Sat:* 9.30*, 12.30, 16.00, 18.30; *Sun/hols:* 13.00, 20.00
*only 15.6-15.9

João Bom — Ponta Delgada
Mon-Fri: 6.00, 7.10, 9.25, 12.30, 15.00, 16.55; *Sat:* 6.00, 7.10, 12.30; *Sun/hols:* 7.05, 14.45

Ponta Delgada — Lagoa — Vila Franca do Campo; Varela & Ca.; journey time about 1h30min
Mon-Fri: 7.00, 7.25, 9.00, 11.00, 12.35, 13.45, 15.00, 16.00, 17.40, 18.10*, 18.30**, 19.00; *Sat:* 8.00, 9.00, 11.00, 12.35, 14.00, 15.00, 17.30; *Sun:* 9.00, 10.00, 16.00+, 18.00
*only Mon-Thur; **only Fri; +only 16.9-14.6

Vila Franca do Campo — Lagoa — Ponta Delgada
Mon-Fri: 6.30, 7.20, 7.40, 8.00, 9.00, 9.30, 9.50, 11.30, 13.00, 14.45, 16.25, 16.55, 17.40; *Sat:* 7.10, 8.00, 9.00, 12.15, 13.45, 15.00+, 17.30, 18.10++; *Sun:* 8.20, 9.55, 12.15, 17.40+, 18.10++
+only 16.9-14.6; ++ only 15.6-14.9

SANTA MARIA

VILA DO PORTO: The central bus station is at the northern end of the village, where the main road forks in front of a green space.

Vila — São Pedro — Ribeira do Engenho — Lagoinhas — Feteiras — Santa Bárbara; journey time 45min
Mon-Sat: 13.30, 18.30*

Santa Bárbara — Feteiras — Lagoinhas — Ribeira do Engenho — São Pedro — Vila
Mon-Sat: 7.00, 14.00*
*not Sat

Vila — Almagreira — Picos — Santo Espírito; journey time 1h 05min
Mon-Fri: 13.30

Santo Espírito — Picos — Almagreira — Vila
Mon-Fri: 14.40

TERCEIRA

ANGRA DO HEROÍSMO: *for departure points, see plan pages 78-79*

Angra — Biscoitos; journey time about 2h
Mon-Fri: 7.45, 10.30, 13.00, 16.00, 17.00, 18.00, 19.00; *Sat:* 7.45, 10.30, 13.00, 16.00, 19.00; *Sun:* 12.00, 16.00, 19.00

Biscoitos — Angra
Mon-Fri: 6.20, 7.20, 9.30, 13.00, 14.30, 17.30; *Sat:* 6.20, 7.20, 9.30, 13.00, 17.30; *Sun:* 10.30, 13.30, 17.30

GRACIOSA

Santa Cruz: Timetables are available at the office of the bus company (Rua da Boa Vista), about 100m from the central square in the direction of Guadalupe. This is also where all the buses depart. There are no buses on Sundays.

Santa Cruz — Praia — F. Mato — Canada Longa — Luz — P. Brancas — B. Branco — Guadalupe — Santa Cruz. This is a circular main route in both directions. If the bus is going clockwise (C), it will take about 10min to Praia, 20min to Canada Longa and 30min to Luz. If the bus is going counter-clockwise, it will take about 30min to Luz, 35min to Canada Longa and 45min to Praia.
Mon-Fri: 7.30* (C), 8.30 (C), 10.30,

11.30, 12.30***, 15.30 (C), 17.00; *Sat:* 8.30 (C), 12.30
*only on school days; **not Thursdays
Thur: 8.15, 12.30* (C), 15.30 (C)
*does not stop everywhere; shorter journey time

Santa Cruz — Ribeirinha; journey time 25min
Mon-Fri: 7.30, 12.30, 15.00

Ribeirinha — Santa Cruz
Mon-Fri: 10.00, 16.30

Luz — Carapacho — Luz; journey time 5min
Only Tue, Fri (Jul/Aug/Sept): 10.45

Carapacho — Luz — Carapacho
Only Tue, Fri (Jul/Aug/Sept): 15.45

FAIAL

HORTA: *for departure points, see town plan page 43*

Horta — Praia do Almoxarife; journey time about 25min
Mon-Fri: 7.15, 12.30, 18.00; *Sat:* 7.15, 12.30

Praia do Almoxarife — Horta
Mon-Fri: 7.20, 13.00, 18.30; *Sat:* 7.40, 13.00

SÃO JORGE

VELAS: Buses depart at the main church. The buses to Calheta and Topo (along the south coast) are at the church, the buses to Rosais and Calheta (via the north coast) are at the petrol station opposite the church.

Velas — Rosais (Igreja) — Rosais (Ponta); journey time 25min
Mon-Fri: 10.00, 14.30; *Sat:* 10.00, 13.00

Rosais (Ponta) — Rosais (Igreja) — Velas
Mon-Fri: 10.25, 14.55; *Sat:* 10.25, 13.25

Velas — Santo António — Calheta
Mon, Tue, Thur: 15.30, 16.10, 17.00; *Wed, Fri:* 8.30, 9.10, 10.00; *Sat:* 14.00, 14.40, 15.30

Calheta — Santo António — Velas
Mon, Tue, Thur: 8.30, 9.30, 10.00; *Wed, Fri:* 15.00, 15.50, 16.30; *Sat:* 8.30, 9.30, 10.00

PICO FERRY

TRANSMAÇOR FAIAL — PICO (15 May to 18 September; daily); journey time 45min. Check if any new timetables have been issued! Note: there are more ferries than listed here. For departure points, see plan page 43.

Horta — Madalena: 7.30, 10.00, 13.00, 15.00, 17.00, 20.00

Madalena — Horta: 8.00, 10.30, 13.30, 15.30, 17.30, 20.30

● Index

This index, arranged alphabetically by islands, contains geographical names only. For all other entries, see Contents, page 3. A page number in *italic type* refers to a map; **bold type** refers to a photograph. Both may be in addition to a text reference on the same page. Approximate pronunciation follows those place names you are likely to have to ask for. Where a syllable is in **bold**, stress that syllable.